FIRST PRINCIPLES FOR MY FIRST ELECTION

A Millennial's Manifesto

ALAN GROVES

NASHVILLE

Copyright © 2012 Alan Groves
All rights reserved.

All rights reserved. No part of this book may be reproduced or transmitted in any form or by any means, including, without limitation, electronically or mechanically, including photocopying, recording, or via any form of information storage and retrieval system, without permission in writing from the author.

About the Author

Alan Groves 18, recently graduated from Ravenwood High School in Williamson County, TN. He is now a Law and Politics major at Freed-Hardeman University. He is a contributor for *TheCollegeConservative.com*, a member of the College Republicans, a board member of the civic organization Linchpins of Liberty, and a member of the Heritage Foundation.

Visit his website at:

http://firstprinciplesformyfirstelection.blogspot.com/

Cover designed by Rachel Guffy (rachellove147.deviantart.com)
Brush Sets by ShiftyJ (shifty.deviantart.com)

Manufactured in the United States of America

ISBN-13: 978-1478314868
ISBN-10: 1478314869

Contents

Acknowledgments 5
Introduction 9
Principle #1 Intellectual Independence 17
Principle #2 Moral Courage 59
Principle #3 Entrepreneurship 103
Principle #4 Self-Reliance 133
Principle #5 American Exceptionalism 157
Principle #6 Civic Duty 195
Appendix 223
About The Author 225
Notes 227

Acknowledgments

It is with joy that I acknowledge and recognize the many friends and family members who made this book possible. As much as this book is a product of my own diligence and creativity, it would be foolish of me not to give credit where credit is due. I would first like to thank my family for their warm words of encouragement. Without their persistent presence to encourage, uplift, and inspire I may have never fully applied my talents. I also thank them for having the patience to tolerate the many hours I spent writing and researching, when I could have been spending time with them.

I also take pleasure in thanking Mr. Kevin Kookogey who, as a friend and mentor, sparked in me the intellectual and moral imagination necessary to discover my first principles. I thank him for introducing me to literary giants and conservative thinkers such as C.S. Lewis and Russell Kirk and for training my mind to see past meaningless political squabbles, and instead to focus on the big Ideas. Without that approach to understanding the first principles of our cherished ordered liberty, this book would be nothing more than another regurgitation of political talking points.

I must also thank a handful of teachers who have personally touched me throughout my high school experience.

Acknowledgments

Though I am highly critical, and sometimes cruel, in my indictment of the institution of public education throughout this book, I must acknowledge my gratitude for the few teachers who, when they observed my hunger for knowledge and thirst for Truth, encouraged and inspired me to satisfy the appetite of my curiosity. Despite the oppressive nature of the public education system and the inherent risk of cultivating a conservative mind, these teachers acted professionally to encourage me in and out of the classroom. Mr. Boyd, my AP European History teacher introduced to me the history of our Western Heritage and provoked in me a curiosity about the past. He also faithfully sponsored my high school's Young Conservatives club for two years, though it may not have been the most popular thing to do. Mr. Landen, my teacher for two years in AP U.S. History and AP Government, also cultivated my interest in history. With his unique personality, which inevitably overflowed with humor and energy, he brought the pages of history to life –teaching us the *story* of history rather than reducing it to boring facts. And like all good story-tellers, he never hesitated to take a break from "learning" to tell us about a special life experience in order to share a lesson in morality.

I also thank Mr. Weaver and Mrs. Hollandsworth –two teachers with very different political philosophies from my own, but who for the most part tolerated my conservative challenges in and out of the classroom. Mr. Weaver, though a math teacher,

Acknowledgments

never denied me the opportunity to debate him on a variety of topics that are typically considered taboo within the halls of a public school. He shared my belief that education truly is about enlightenment and that the best way to achieve a higher level of understanding about the world was through classical conversation. Though we usually arrived at different conclusions, we challenged each other's thinking and inspired one another to pursue the Truth. Similarly, Mrs. Hollandsworth, my AP English teacher for two years, tolerated and even embraced the energy that I brought to the classroom. She appreciated the fact that I brought a new perspective to the discussion, knowing just as well as I that most students would be content to sit in a circle and, like mindless zombies, agree on everything just to make a good grade. She also allowed me my first taste of great literature.

All these people have contributed to the production of this book in some form or another, whether through their personal relationship with me and their influence on my thinking or by their technical support in my book's physical publication. To each of them I owe untold gratitude. Only God Himself remains to be recognized. Without His guidance, protection, and divine intervention, none of this would be possible. I thank Him for introducing all of these people into my life and for working through them to edify me. Most of all I thank Him for bequeathing to me (and to all of humanity) that "little spark of celestial fire called conscience," from which I truly derive my first principles.

Introduction

"For though by this time you ought to be teachers, you need someone to teach you again the first principles *of the oracles of God; and you have come to need milk and not solid food. For everyone who partakes only of milk is unskilled in the word of righteousness, for he is a babe. But solid food belongs to those who are of full age, that is, those who by reason of use have their senses exercised to discern both good and evil."* –Heb. 5:12-14 (NKJV)

My name is Alan Groves. A recent graduate of Ravenwood High School I, along with tens of thousands of teenagers and young adults across the nation, have reached an age where we are now deemed "legal" by society, and thus we have earned our glorious independence and the responsibilities

First Principles for my First Election

that come with it. What an exciting time! For the first 18 years of my life, I have grown up in middle TN, where there's not much a kid can do to change the world. In fact, kids anywhere have a hard time changing the world. Though built up by fantastic hopes and utopian dreams of ending world hunger, ending poverty, and securing world peace, kids are powerless in the eyes of the law. Whether five, ten, twelve, or even seventeen, there is little one can do to achieve change.

For those of us who have crossed that societal-imposed threshold with our 18th birthday (or soon will), entering into adulthood, that precedent is about to change. We *will* be able to make a difference. No longer will "I can't make a difference" be an acceptable excuse. When we turn 18, we win our right to vote and with it, the opportunity to put theory into action. Instead of learning about politics and government, copying notes, and taking tests, we will be able to participate in the political process ourselves. In a hands-on approach, we can bring our creative potential, our personal experiences, our values and our principles to the table and work towards making America a better, freer, nation.

It is not news to me, however, that politics is not the most popular thing in the world or anything about which most young people are very energetic and passionate. In fact I think that goes for the whole country. Who *likes* politics? At the thought of politics, most people (including myself) get a

Introduction

mental image of a bunch of old Washington elitists arguing senselessly with other Washington elitists simply because of the "R" or "D" after their name. Whether it is watching red-faced, high-blood pressured partisans bickering on cable T.V, discovering politicians involved with sex and scandal in the news, or finding that some backroom deal has been brokered behind close doors, it is safe to say that Americans generally have a negative outlook toward politics.

Teenagers and young adults are no exception. I know good and well that the last thing on our minds is politics. We are preoccupied with sports, our cars, our friends, dating, and perhaps a few of us bookworms are up to our heads in academics as we prepare for college. The last thing most of us want to do is keep up with politics, defend our beliefs, and risk the chance of making a few enemies along the way. I get that. I understand.

I am a young adult as well. I understand the challenges and difficulties that teenagers and young people go through, and I hope that this book will bring a unique perspective in that respect. It is still to be accounted for, though, that however young we may be, we are still adults. That means we have certain responsibilities just as all other adults do. We cannot be babied our whole lives. As much as some wish it were, this is not Neverneverland. We cannot be kids forever. We cannot be pampered, spoiled, and just expect all the troubles of the

First Principles for my First Election

world to disappear. This does not mean that we cannot have fun. It does not mean we cannot spend time with our friends or focus on our studies. But the fact is, if our nation does not get its act together, and if our generation fails to lead, none of those things will matter anymore. As disgusting, frustrating, and confusing as politics can be, it affects every aspect of our lives. If freedom's flame grows dim on our watch, we will suffer. The luxuries and comforts that so many of us enjoy, will be no more if the very liberty that provided for them is taken for granted.

In spite of those dire consequences, there will be many that won't know exactly whom to vote for, or how to get involved (until they have reconnected with their first principles). Others will look down upon my generation and pessimistically declare our incompetence for solving the problems of tomorrow.

I believe in the great potential of my generation-The Millennials. We have been branded as a lazy generation, obsessed with technology that has no respect for God or our fellow man. But in fact, I have faith that it will be our generation that will bring this country out of the slum-a slum our parents and grandparents created. I believe that behind the gadgets and gizmos lies a creative and innovative generation of young American citizens. I do not believe that we are

Introduction

inherently any different than any generation to go before us. Human nature does not change with the calendar. [1a]

Our whole lives we have been told that we could do anything if we set our mind to it. However when it comes to politics and fixing the state of our Union, we are told that the situation is helpless. *The system is broken. The American Dream is dead. It cannot be fixed-let alone by us.* I deny every word. American ingenuity still exists and in some ways more so with the new technologies of the 21st century. As made apparent by the presidential election of 2008, it is the era of "yes, we can!" Millennials are bursting with positive energy and buzzing to participate in our political system. However, it is true that this burning passion for hope and change has been void of any foundational principles or moral truths to justify such dramatic change. And in a sweeping feeling of buyer's remorse, Millennials who previously voted in 2008 for President Obama in record numbers now regret their impulsive and emotion-driven vote. [2b] His campaign was

---

[a] The "slum" to which I refer consists of the 14 trillion ($14,000,000,000,000+) national debt (16 trillion when accounting for the new raise in the debt ceiling) and a 8.4% unemployment rate. According to the United States Department of Labor, the unemployment rate is 23.7% for 16-19 year olds, as of this writing. These wretched economic conditions are facts of life and the reflection of wrongs made by older generations, not by Millennials. This "slum," however is not limited to the unfortunate economic conditions of the day, but also encompasses the degrading moral standing of our culture caused by an older generation's neglect of faith and morality in exchange for a secular value system.

[b] About 66% of Millennials voted for President Obama in 2008. Shortly before the 2010 midterm elections, polls showed that the young voters' approval of the President had drastically dropped from 60% to 44%. This translated into a more divided youth vote in the 2010 elections. While still left-leaning, the youth only voted Democratic by a margin

First Principles for my First Election

artificially built up by a host of false promises and carried forward by alluring fantasies of hope and change. Yet, the chains of debt continue to be forged, our economy is teetering on collapse, the "international community" still does not approve of America while Islamic extremists are more powerful than ever, and the promise of transparency and honesty was shattered with a bitterly fought health care bill and a "jam-it-through" style lame duck session. [3c]

It is true that our generation was born into different circumstances; we have inherited a different culture, and are unique in our outlook on life, and certainly, though by no fault of our own, we have grown up without a solid foundation of principles and values. For this reason, the coming election is of the utmost importance and it is a chance for the Millennials to right a major wrong. Nearly four years have passed since the last election, and for the many Millennials, like me, who are only just now of voting-age, this is a chance to start off on good footing. It is a chance to discover our first principles and apply them.

---

of 56% as opposed to the 66% that voted for Pres. Obama, reflecting a shift in the minds in a significant number of pragmatic and aware groups of Millennials.

[c] The shackles of "chains of debt" continue to be forged as Republicans and Democrats continue spending more money and continue to raise the legal limit of what they can borrow. On August 2nd, 2011 a bi-partisan agreement was made to raise the debt ceiling by $2.1 Trillion in exchange for an empty promise that an unconstitutional "super committee" in Congress will make a mere $1 Trillion in spending cuts over 10 years. Also, polls show that the U.S. still lacks even a majority of approval from the international community, despite President Obama's election. In fact, after the initial bump in approval after his election, the U.S.'s world-wide approval has declined since he took office in 2009.

Introduction

My generation has been born into a culture of apathy and ambivalence. Many are still undecided about where they stand on certain issues and are confused when it comes to making politically aware decisions. Many will just sit out this historic election. This book is meant to combat that apathy and to call the Millennials to action. This is our chance to channel our energy, our optimism, and our ingenuity head first against the political machine. This is our chance to rebel against the establishment and to defeat a formidable foe. This is our chance to defend our liberty and make a good name for the Millennials. This is our chance to return control of our future to its rightful owners-WE THE PEOPLE. It begins with having a few First Principles for an important First Election.

The following pages are meant to be a restoration of old principles, not new, and a renewal of time-tested truths that are indeed self-evident. These principles are the key, not only in the casting of one's first vote, but to the future of our nation. The problems of the 21st century will not be solved by politics or by new "progressive" ideas. They will be solved by an innovative, creative generation of Millennials who have reconnected with the history of their nation's founding, the moral foundations of civil society, and the importance of individual liberty. The moral and economic prosperity of America will only be restored by these ideals, these first principles.

Principle #1

Intellectual Independence

It is a fact that the Left has taken captive an overwhelming number of Millennials in recent years. As mentioned earlier, *two-thirds* of my generation voted for a presidential candidate who was previously voted the most liberal member of the Senate.[4a] Certainly the Left has won the majority of Millennials, even more have slid into an uncaring ambivalence, and few are conservatives. What are the ramifications for such a dramatic shift in the electorate?

---

[a] In addition to his overtly-liberal tendencies, President Obama could boast little of his record when it came to demonstrating his experience –or lack thereof. Prior to serving the first two years of his term before running for the Presidency, Mr. Obama had voted "present" (neither yea, nor nay) a whopping 130 times in the Illinois State Senate. Critics claim that this flimsy voting record revealed the fact the senator wanted to conceal his true radical colors. Yet, it was perhaps because of this thin resume that Millennials took the bait in the 2008 presidential election.

First Principles for my First Election

If this trend continues and remains unchecked, our nation will wither into a chaotic state of entitlement and pure ignorance as our generation replaces the leaders of the present.[b] WE are the future! We must, as every generation has the responsibility of doing, grow leaders and nurture their character, teach them history, encourage them to lead, and then emulate their service ourselves. I am part of this generation and this is my responsibility too. Yet, the current system provides for none of these virtues.

The present establishment is designed to stifle individual creativity and to prevent exceptional leaders from emerging. The professional Left has invaded the world of academia and has remade it into a bureaucratic stronghold that at first glance seems faultless and impenetrable. In the arena of public education, liberals have begun the transformation of American society that takes direct aim at molding the next generation in conformity with its utopian goals.

These goals do not include the encouragement of a new generation of leaders, learned in history, character, and moral courage. No, the goals of the Left have more to do with raising

---

[b] The economic and societal breakdown of Europe foreshadows this fact. After Greece fell under the pressure of its entitlement state it descended into chaotic violence and dangerous riots. Likewise, Great Britain is beginning to see the effects of a broken economy as demonstrated by the London riots this past summer. Even the U.S. has experienced an outbreak of "flashmobs" in urban areas in the North where gangs organize mass-robberies and other acts of crime in large numbers to ensure success and avoidance of law enforcement.

Intellectual Independence

a generation that is self-aware of "inequality" and is dedicated to the advocacy of social and economic justice. In their quest against inequality, the Left has taken to the extreme. They rail against the unequal distribution of wealth and preach against the sins of capitalism with a spirit and fervor that rivals the most radical fire and brimstone sermons. They present the radical philosophies of progressivism, socialism, Marxism as viable solutions to the economic grievances of our day. They teach a biased version of American history, in which the Founders are reduced to wealthy and greedy aristocrats and the Constitution as a product of their selfish ambitions. Meanwhile we are taught that FDR saved the nation from the toils of the capitalist-induced Great Depression. We are taught that the 1960's was a victory for social progress and diversity. We are ridiculed if we do not accept homosexual marriage or if we do not believe that college admission offices should judge people by the color of their skin. Science is worshipped as if a religion and global warming alarmists constantly assault us with their eco-friendly, go-green agenda. We are taught that God and religion are outdated superstitions of our parents. The Bible is fictitious and *The Origin of Species* is Holy.

We all know the routine. We all know the garbage. We have all been immersed in it from childhood, and we all nodded our heads like good little students in perfect

First Principles for my First Election

submission. We took the test. We got the grade. We moved on.

That has to change. This liberal takeover of educational institutions severely threatens the future prosperity of our nation, as an entire generation is being used like lab rats for the liberal elite's social experiments. Their agenda threatens creativity and punishes intellectual diversity. It stifles dissenting views and silences opposing voices. It hinders innovation and ignores achievement. Something has to be done.

Of all the principles which will move us forward as a nation, intellectual independence will be the key to unlocking the shackles on individual liberty. We the students and graduates must declare our independence from the Machine.

What is the Machine? It is the Machine that has kept us in the dark intellectually and kept us from being all that we can be. The Machine has transformed education into a mechanical, repetitive, boring process of flooding the minds of kids with political propaganda which is to be tediously memorized and regurgitated. The consequence of deviation, in word or deed, from the Will of the Machine is to accept academic fatality. Diversity of opinion, thought, or faith is not permitted by the Machine –the Machine of indoctrination and submission.

The effects of the Left's strangle on education is evident. The overwhelming majority of our generation has *fallen* for

Intellectual Independence

this bologna! After years of propaganda and enticing incentives, many have taken the bait. They have no opinion of their own and no ability to think for themselves. Without any intellectual backbone, they lean on the ignorant and superficial teachings of their youth. These are the future leaders of our generation. But how can the blind lead the blind?

Their policies, while professing progress, are merely social experiments –not policies bent on genuine reform or economic innovation. These policies reflect the "group-think" mentality of the era, which inevitably lead to damaging effects on the nation by these ill-focused policies. The politics of the youth is now collectively driven and resembles more of a fad culture rather than an in depth philosophical discussion.

These fads include the "go-green" movement, political correctness, anti-Americanism, and collectivist economic policy. These are political fads which originate from the Machine-mere pieces of propaganda designed to appeal to a younger generation. However, these agendas are not rooted in any universal principles or general truths. They are nothing more than feel-good policies which promote self-righteousness and arrogance.

Many young people have easily become hypnotized by the raging emotionalism of the Left. They support policies that depend upon the empathy and emotion rather than logic or reason. Often times, these emotional ploys are nothing but

First Principles for my First Election

hidden attempts of the left to capture a certain voting bloc (the Millennials), and not about promoting genuine change.

Empirical evidence supports the feel-good motivation of the brainwashed youth. Yale University and George Mason University conducted a survey on the issue of dedication to the environment (an issue extremely popular with the youth).[5] The results revealed an obvious, but not surprising trend: while many of the pro-green initiatives were widely and enthusiastically supported, few of the respondents admitted to actually putting them into practice in their own personal lives.

For instance, when asked if one supported the use of public transportation or carpooling instead of private transportation, 62% said yes. However, when asked whether or not the respondent actually did this, only 10% could affirm their dedication. Likewise, while half of those questioned supported reusable shopping bags at the grocery store, only a third actually used them. Even the hallmark of the green-movement –recycling- was only actually practiced by 51% of those participating in the survey. It is a general and widely accepted trend that while people, particularly students, support these good intentioned and seemingly altruistic policies, they don't have the backbone to put them into practice. The only logical explanation for this is that of a thoughtless and intellectually bankrupt generation that relies on emotion rather than reason. It makes them feel good.

Intellectual Independence

There are numerous examples of this raving emotionalism. The youth is artificially puffed up by ideas of eliminating inequality once and for all and feel that government intervention is justified on any level if interceding in the name of social justice. Whether it is helping the poor through government handouts, caring for the children through public education, or using the federal government to protect "discriminated" social minorities, the youth's support of these initiatives largely rests in irrational emotion and not principled conviction.

Emotional appeal can hardly be considered a new tactic of the Left. In reality, it is as old as time itself. Man is and forever will be a slave to his emotions and his passions. Ever since his Fall, man has been led astray by the smoothed tongued Deceiver who loves to take the form of our most basic desires: be it our quest for perfection, our physical impulses, or our sense of justice. It is the latter mode of deceit that has seduced the Millennial generation, just as it has so many others before us. We are built up with fanciful dreams and utopian goals and assured that government is the only means of achieving those ends. We cannot refuse the power of our passions, and in the name of social justice we are led astray.

The life of Orestes Brownson (1803-1876) is a tribute to the fact of the Left's dangerous pathos as he himself documents. Intellectually confused from childhood, Brownson

First Principles for my First Election

grew up into the world searching for a sense of true Justice. More than anything, his soul longed for intellectual certitude and conviction in an idea or set of ideas that satisfied his internal passion for social justice. In this quest he experimented throughout his youth and early adult life with different philosophies, ideologies and theologies. He changed his religion about seven times from Congregationalism, to Presbyterianism, to Universalism, to humanitarianism, to Unitarianism, to Transcendentalism, and finally deciding on Catholicism. He was active in socialist undertakings and an avid reader of Robert Owen and Fanny Wright. For a whole year he became a militant atheist and a revolutionary conspirator.[c]

Brownson wrote about the intellectual struggles of his youth and especially the perilous nature of the Left's raving emotionalism which was responsible for his downfall. Now he reads like a prophet:

"Socialism conceals from the undiscriminating multitude its true character, and, appealing to the dominant sentiment of the age and to some of our strongest natural inclinations, and passions, it asserts itself with terrific power…Men are assimilated to it by all the power of their own nature, and by

---

[c] It is interesting to note that Brownson was a militant socialist and atheist even before the name of Marx was even known, who didn't publish his *Communist Manifesto* until 1848.

Intellectual Independence

all their reverence for religion. Their very faith and charity are perverted, and their noblest sympathies and their sublimest hopes are made subservient to their basest passions and their most groveling propensities. Here is the secret of the strength of Socialism, and here is the principal source of its danger."[6]

Brownson came to understand this and rejected and repented of the road he had taken. He converted to Catholicism and began to discover the genius of American order. For the rest of his life he publicly defended and promoted his revelation of the true "Just Society" –one that manifests itself through a limited government that protects individual liberty and equal opportunity all the while supported by a religious citizenry and holds the sentiments of personal responsibility, charity, and love for one's neighbor dear.

Brownson's struggles are the same struggles we face today. While the powerful and influential leaders may not be sitting in a dark, pipe-smoke filled room dreaming up ways to deceive the Millennial generation, their emotional ploys and reliance upon ignorance and blind servitude are inherent to the very nature of their ideology, as Brownson notes. It would be wise for this generation to heed the words of one who has already walked the perilous path.

First Principles for my First Election

We have to understand the games that are being played. The Machine has fed us their superficial agenda in hopes to capture an assured segment of the population who would support their political cause. Playing us for fools, they have exploited our emotions and guilt-tripped us into supporting faddish policies meanwhile depriving many of their full intellectual potential. It's Orestes Brownson all over again.

Of course, all this makes sense once you understand that to political elites, education is not about enlightenment or challenging the mind, heart, and soul; it is about indoctrination of feeble minded and intellectually defenseless children.[d] Progressives have a history of elitism, while simultaneously trumpeting the common good. To them, the public is stupid, ignorant, and incapable of self-government. However, because *they* are a highly intelligent and well educated class of citizens, they can easily decide what is best for the common good. Thus, they must seek every effort to manage your daily life for you (since you are too stupid). This is seen in the modern political arena through expansive and bureaucratic "administration," through regulatory scheming, and through economic "central planning." However, the best example of progressive elitism can be seen in education.

---

[d] Understand, it is not I that think us children. According to the Left, we are only intellectual infants –stupid, ignorant, and incapable of making our own choices without their proper guidance. In fact, according to Obamacare, a "child" is defined as being 30 or younger!

Intellectual Independence

Institutions of learning are ideal for progressive elites to exercise their desired complete, dictatorial rule over others. Who better to test their radical ideas upon, than the energetic and rebellious youth who bite at the heels to break away from established traditions, ideas, and lines of thinking? This is not a conspiracy. College kids witness this first hand. According to the Washington Post, the Left has *monopolized* their control over higher education. "72 percent of those teaching at American universities and colleges are liberal and 15 percent are conservative." From here the facts become more grim. "The disparity is even more pronounced at the most elite schools, where, according to the study, 87 percent of faculty are liberal and 13 percent are conservative." Interestingly enough, the reported study found that, "the most left-leaning departments are English literature, philosophy, political science and religious studies, where at least 80 percent of the faculty say they are liberal and no more than 5 percent call themselves conservative..." How appropriate! The areas of greatest intellectual importance, politics and religion, are controlled by a monopoly of liberal, out of touch academics![7]

This is extremely concerning. Or could it be a mere coincidence that an entire generation of young people just happens to be falling in line with the progressive machine after graduating college? Could it also be a coincidence that this generation has become hostile with increasing intensity

First Principles for my First Election

toward organized religion?[8e] No. The only logical explanation is that an entire generation Americans has been wrongly influenced by a corrupted and monopolized education system, which is littered with liberal professors who eagerly thrust their own opinions on their students. Anyone who denies this is a fool. There is simply no other force with the power and influence to roll back centuries of established principles, traditions, and moral precepts.

This is no accident. The Left knows good and well which subjects are important for crafting and molding a new generation of ideological foot soldiers. They understand that they need to hijack the "humanities," which include history, religion, speech, and the legal areas of higher education in order to have a medium to assert their emotional propaganda. Only be infiltrating these areas and instilling in their students an interest in "social justice" can the Left achieve their ends. Teach history majors that America is evil and convince them that government has a responsibility to actively engage in social affairs to right past wrongs. Teach economics majors that capitalism is evil and convince them that government should redistribute the wealth more "equally." Teach political science majors that they should pursue a degree in law so they can turn courts into active chambers of social justice. Teach

---

[e] 1 in 4 Millennials now report no religious affiliation. This number has more than doubled in 20 years and far exceeds the percent of atheists nationwide - 16% (which accounts for all ages).

Intellectual Independence

philosophy majors that there is no divine Truth and that everything is relative.

Allan Levite observes in his book *Guilt, Blame, and Politics*, those careers in academia actually breed the distinction between out of touch academics and regular people. According to Levite,

"Academics, especially in the less worldly areas such as art, literature, and the social sciences, may also be affected by their own remoteness from the mundane environment of production and commerce, as well as by the greater extent to which their erudition separates and shelters them from the rest of the world...Scholars in the humanities and the social sciences are even further removed from the workaday world than are other academics, and are therefore more likely to favor social leveling."[9]

In other words, because of the nature of their careers, members of the intelligentsia have a natural propensity to fall prey to political arrogance and elitism. Because they are sheltered from mainstream America, and live with their minds in the clouds, they have the tendency to dream up big schemes of social justice and economic equality –dabbling in theory rather than principled facts and historical precedent.

First Principles for my First Election

This is not the first time in history when the world of academia has been targeted by the Left. In fact, leftists have a long history of infiltrating the intelligentsia in order to assault the minds of the rising generation. I have had the privilege of knowing one lady in particular who suffered under these conditions even to a greater extent than we do here in the States. I met Galina Koval at my church, but her history and background was far removed from my small hometown of Franklin, TN. Born in 1937 in Leningrad (now St Petersburg), Galina grew up in the communist Soviet Union. Daughter of an abusive father and broken family, Galina's early family life was difficult. Her father's position, though, secured her an "education" (if it can be called that) and a future career in teaching at the university level. Thus, Galina Koval spent much of her life in the world of intellegenstia –both as a student at the University of Marxism-Leninism and as a professor of English at a university.

Galina calls these educational establishments "ideological institutions" in her memoir *From Darkness to Great Light*. She explains how the political elite had co-opted the learning process and instead substituted their own "Soviet media and propaganda." She writes of how education dwarfed into a system of indoctrination and obedience, rather than a discussion and honest pursuit of truth. After fleeing to the United States she often reflects upon the lack of intellectual

Intellectual Independence

diversity and absence of freedom of thought. She also describes how so many victims of the tyranny of the Soviet Union were deprived of their individual thought and yet lives in ignorance because of a fear to ask questions and challenge authority.

"If a person thinks like everybody else and like the government wants him to think, he can live like a blind person, who has never seen light and does not miss it. But if a person begins thinking independently, differently, if he realizes that the system is wrong and human beings should not live like they are forced to live, that they should be free to make their choices..."[10]

This is almost prophetic, considering this was written about a regime half-way across the world nearly 50 years ago. Yet, it speaks to the problem of indoctrination and intellectual conformity in the universities and "ideological institutions" of America today. It would be wise to heed the advice of Ms. Koval to become individuals who think independently and develop the ability to think critically –sorting among political fads, biased teaching, and the truth.

Yes, the Left knows which subjects are important. Unfortunately, conservatives usually pursue careers in business, manufacturing, technology, and construction. By

First Principles for my First Election

nature, conservatives aren't really energetic about forcing students into intellectual straightjackets. Even those that are intellectually well-rounded and quite interested in law, philosophy, and history have no inherent desire to force their ideas or opinions on someone else. Most conservatives –like most people- prefer to live at peace with themselves and society. We just want to live alone and we want others to respect our privacy. In this day in age however, that excuse just does not cut it. The forces on the Left are drastically changing public sentiment through the universities and other institutions of higher education. They are erasing history, distorting truth, and smothering intellectual independence. Our defense is not as strong as their offense. So perhaps, it is time that trend should change. More conservatives should pursue these areas of interest if not to pass down their wisdom, than to prevent the truth from distortion or utter annihilation. Conservatives should get back to the books and resurrect that old idea of what used to be considered an education.

Once upon a time, education, especially higher education, was created to satisfy the inherent curiosity of mankind-to pursue truth. The idea of "truth" was thought to be universal, comprising of the highest levels of knowledge which gives understanding not only of the natural sciences of the world, but of history, philosophy, and religion –a grand reconciliation of all things that are true. With the Sword of Truth, education

Intellectual Independence

would empower the *individual* and would lead to worldly enlightenment and also spiritual understanding. This used to be called a "liberal arts education." The purpose was individual and personal and its objectives wide and lofty. Of this aspect of education, Dr. Larry Arnn writes, "The understanding of human nature also carries implication for the purpose of the governing structure of education. Liberal education is the study of ends –of the things for the sake of which choices are made and lives are lived. The Founders in their political understanding point up toward the permanent, the final, and the divine, in the same way that liberal education does."[11] Or has Russell Kirk would say, "The permanent things."

When John Dewey, the "father of modern education," transformed that traditional institution in the early 20th century, he dramatically shifted its focus and purpose. As a progressive John Dewy was not concerned with Truth –which to progressives was only relative and something that changed with circumstances (Millennials today call this postmodernism). Neither was Dewy concerned with the empowerment of the individual. No, to this man education was about the *collective*. It was about *democracy*.

He writes:

First Principles for my First Election

"I believe that the school is primarily a social institution. Education being a social process, the school is simply that form of community life in which all those agencies are concentrated that will be most effective in bringing the child to share in the inherited resources of the race, and to use his own powers for social ends."[12]

Here we can see that to Dewey, who forever changed the system of education in America, believed education to be about empowering society, not the individual. In this respect Dewey is responsible for refiguring education to mimic the system of the Prussians and later the Soviets. There was not emphasis on truth or individual enlightenment. According to Dewey, students should not work hard, study, cultivate and explore their own talents for their own benefit, but for the *community*.

Now, in 21st century America, we are left with a system of education rooted in the collectivist mindset of Dewey. However, after the 1960's leftists radicals came under the impression that the system was not working quickly enough to promote social change. Their ideas were simply being ignored and trampled upon. Thus, a militant movement to stifle dissent and freedom of thought was undergo. The academic elites knew what was best for the collective. They understood. Their ideas just were not being accepted. Therefore, keeping with

Intellectual Independence

the social goals of Dewey, they added their own dictatorial element to the mix.

In recent decades, the workings of the education system can be described in one word: FEAR. In order to insure that their social goals are fulfilled, the left has instituted fear tactics which smother intellectual diversity and freedom of thought. It's their way or the highway.

The culture of fear embedded in the American education system cannot be understated. For this reason, scholars such as Dr. Richard Weaver have written extensively on the topic of fear and the various ways in which progressive policies have overseen the decay of American education. With an unforgiving forcefulness, Dr. Weaver excoriates these trends in *Ideas Have Consequences*:

"…it is precisely because we have lost our grasp of the nature of knowledge that we have nothing to educate with for the salvation of our order. Americans certainly cannot be reproached for failing to invest adequately in the hope that education would prove redemption. They have built numberless high schools, lavish in equipment, only to see them, under the prevailing scheme of values, turned into social centers and institutions for improving the personality, where teachers, living in fear of constituents, dare not enforce scholarship. They have built colleges on an equal scale, only

First Principles for my First Election

to see them turned into playgrounds for grown-up children or centers of vocationalism and professionalism. Finally, they have seen pragmatists, as if in peculiar spite against the very idea of hierarchy, endeavoring to turn classes into democratic forums, where the teacher is only a moderator, and no one offends by presuming to speak with superior knowledge."[13]

How right he is! Slamming the utter incompetence of the post-progressive American education system, Weaver criticizes the superb waste of money on high schools which have been transformed into "social centers" where kids can "improve the personality" and colleges which have become nothing more than "playgrounds for grown-up children." He also hits the nail on the head when he notes the instrument of fear common in public institutions of education.

How many times can you remember that you were afraid to speak up against something your teacher might have said that violated your principles or even something that was a blatant lie? How many essays have you written where you were forced to take the side of your teacher so that you would get a good grade, even while sacrificing your principles? Some have probably written essays rooted in the firm conviction their principles and suffered anyway! Then, on the other side of the coin, there are *teachers* who suffer from the intimidation and fear tactics of the Left, as Mr. Weaver points

Intellectual Independence

out. In some cases it is downright comical to see teachers trying to jump through hoops of political correctness just too avoid criticism by students, parents, or administration. Whether it's a history teacher side-stepping any points of controversy, or an English teacher who uses "his or her" religiously, or a Chemistry teacher who puts up a non-religious "Chemist-tree" to avoid any hurt feelings, sometimes the culture of fear can inspire quite comical results.[f] It becomes much more serious however, when a teacher fears to deviate from a rigid curriculum, leaving the shining nuggets of truth undiscovered within the *true* pages of history. Even more concerning is when the teacher is in fact the instigator of such fear tactics and thus uses his position as a bully pulpit.

I have had personal experiences with this. As I mentioned earlier, I have had, as most kids probably have, certain English teachers who have banned essay topics for things are just "too controversial" or in some cases "too religious." One teacher in fact, called the tone of my research paper on the history of American Feminism "inflammatory and offensive." (I didn't know historical facts could be offensive.) I absolutely love the teacher and her class and I think we have a good student-teacher relationship, but I think I hit a reflexive nerve present in all people, not just teachers, that retaliates negatively when their opinions are challenged by facts. Even the fairest of

---

[f] All of these examples have actually happened to me!

First Principles for my First Election

teachers, such as this particular English teacher (who must be fair to some degree if she has put up with me for this long!), can make biased judgments –even if unintentionally. The problem comes when those biased judgments and sometimes intentional judgments by teachers induce fear and subservience in the hearts of Millennials who then cower beneath the imposing shadow of the Machine.

I have also had the unfortunate experience in questioning my biology teacher on matters of evolution. Though I respect the teacher herself and in fact have a favorable opinion of her personality, she was indeed the mouthpiece of the Left. Though to her credit, her job mandates that she teach certain material, it does not prohibit the exposure to alternative and well-founded scientific ideas –which she did not do. I was left with one alternative: to be the voice of reason and honest objection and to vigilantly pursue truth. Though it took courage and sometimes a good dose of embarrassment, I bravely asked the questions I thought should be asked. When my teacher responded, I respected her answer (sometimes accepting it, sometimes not accepting it) and pursued my line of questioning. To my surprise, my confrontation with the establishment (again not the teacher herself, who was very honest and respectful, but rather the ideas she represented and the fear which they induced) was well accepted by my peers, many of whom were inspired by my boldness and who

Intellectual Independence

themselves chimed in during the discussion. My other clashes with the Machine are numerous and I will explore more of them throughout the book. Each instance is a result of fear, whether on the part of the student or the teacher.

My personal clashes with the establishment do not bother me much. I am firm in my convictions and am not easily intimidated. In fact, I have taken the offensive approach and pro-actively get involved in my school and community to combat that culture of fear that smothers dissent and prevents voices from being heard. After the President of my high school's Young Republicans graduated, I ran for his office and was unanimously elected. Under my leadership, the club voted to change its name to the Young Conservatives and we decided to take the club into a new direction. We would concern ourselves more with rediscovering our first principles and provide a forum for healthy debate. For the first time in the clubs history, we hosted several open-forum debates to come and discuss hot-button issues so that all sides could be heard without the annoyance or fear imposed by an administrator or a teacher. Students are allowed to open up in these debates and express whatever opinion they like.

Under my leadership, we also host several guest speakers including local elected officials such as our state senator and state representative, in order to self-educate ourselves on the process of government. This in depth analysis and one on one

First Principles for my First Election

discussion with public officials builds the esteem of the club and allows an opportunity for hands on learning that we seldom get to experience in the classroom.

Our club also applies our principles of charity and love for our neighbors by actively participating in local charities. Last year we sponsored a children's book drive at our high school which collected over 300 children's books to be sent to an underprivileged elementary school.

I am also the board member of the civic organization Linchpins of Liberty –founded by my own mentor and friend Kevin Kookogey. The goal of this organization is to "challenge the imagination of the rising generation" by getting Millennials involved in reading the right books and growing in the knowledge of civic and religious liberty protected by our republican, constitutional form of government.

Through these activities I seek to practice what I preach – putting the culture of fear on the defensive by being bold, active, and visible with my conservative values. Because actions speak louder than words, I hope that others may take inspiration from my aspirations and accomplishments and make them their own.

Unfortunately, most of my peers and most Millennials in general are not as confident in themselves or their convictions. What pains me is to see friends of mine fold under the pressure and submit to the machine. One of my friends (who

Intellectual Independence

will rename nameless for the purposes of this book) has been heavily involved in the Young Conservatives at my school. However, he takes extreme and in some cases embarrassing measures to hide his political affiliation from teachers. He requests that I do not mention his name when talking about our club and requests not to be mentioned on our club's Facebook page. The latter request came when another teacher, a friend of his, saw a picture of my friend on Facebook at an event hosted by the Heritage Foundation. The teacher scolded him for his actions and was surprised that he could possibly be a conservative. The incident shouldn't have been surprising; this teacher was known to be very open and sometimes aggressive about his political views. He even displayed Obama signs in the classroom during the last election cycle until students and parents complained to the administration.

Nevertheless, my friend was very hurt, but also conflicted. He is not ashamed of his beliefs, but is afraid of possible repercussions and encounters with teachers of malevolent intention. While I don't share his concern or fear of unprofessional teachers, it is very unfortunate that some students feel the need to hide their true sentiments.

Another friend told me about how she was pressured by her teacher into changing the topic of her research paper – which was originally going to be on the NYC Mosque debate –instead to how Muslims are victims of unfair stereotypes and

First Principles for my First Election

discrimination in the then ongoing Mosque debate. Though she held a view categorically opposed to such an argument, she bit her lip and wrote the paper. She got an A, but to what avail? She sacrificed truth for a grade. I do not blame her however. I blame the teacher and the culture of fear which his actions represent. It was the culture of fear (working through the teacher) that induced the fear which made her change her topic –not her own conscience.

One (of the many) encounters I've had with the thought-police occurred in my sophomore year of high school. I confronted the administration to request the free distribution of political literature (as required under school rules). The occasion was "Earth Day." Our club wanted to distribute written material provided by the Young America's Foundation which exposed the "green movement" as leftist propaganda. The "leaflets" of paper contained factual information such as quotes from high ranking government officials and even the Communist Party USA's platform which revealed their intention to use the green movement as a means of expanding government control over the lives of average citizens. The project we wanted to undertake was fact-based, educational, and provided an opinion not often heard within the ranks of left-leaning Millennials. We wanted to pass out these fliers hoping to show people that not everyone bought into the eco-garbage which had been thrust upon them by their teachers

Intellectual Independence

and fellow peers. Unfortunately the administration would not allow it. *It was too controversial. What if a parent called and complained to the administration? Too many things could go wrong...*

I do not blame the administration. In fact, I know many of the administrators to be very conservative folks. It is the system. The system of fear. The Left has cultivated this sentiment of fear and it has infected our schools; I can attest.

The last aspect of fear in our education system that I would like to discuss is in the fear of ostracism. Many students have already fallen prey to the collectivist mindset. Thus, when they have an opinion that is at odds with their friends or teachers they automatically assume that they are wrong. They rely on collective wisdom. The teachers are the experts and if one's classmates are all in agreement, they must be right. *What will my friends think if they find out I don't buy into global warming? What will they think if they find out I'm pro-life?* The social repercussions could be devastating. Depending on the situation, the issue, and the people involved, political discussions can turn very sour very quickly. Coupled with the youth's "group-think" mentality and fad culture, it takes courage to overcome the fear of ostracism.

The problem is not for students like me who have already made up their minds. The problem lay in the fact that campus life, in grade school and in universities, smothers dissenters

First Principles for my First Election

and stifles diversity of thought. While schools bend over backwards to insure appreciation for "cultural diversity," there is little to no emphasis on *intellectual* diversity. Fears about getting sued over discrimination lawsuits are much more urgent than ensuring a well-rounded, intellectually independent, and politically informed citizenry, right?

Many kids have, and will continue, to be educated without being challenged intellectually. They will be fed liberal propaganda and will be forced under boot to the throat scare tactics to regurgitate it. They will not have the opportunity to dissent, to disagree, or to develop their own principles and opinions. If the current trends in public education continue, upon graduation we will all turn out to be factory items, in perfect uniform and intellectual conformity, rather than as unique individuals. As British statesman and philosopher Disraeli once said of his own political opponents on the Left, "By their system of state education all would be thrown into the same mint, and all would come out with the same impress and superscription."[14] The Left craves conformity. They hate individuality. What would happen if, God forbid, Millennials could think for themselves! Schools should be centers of disagreement! They should foster and encourage debate. Only through open debate can ideas be fully explored, accepted, or refuted –In plain light, not under the cover of fear and darkness.

Intellectual Independence

Free speech is of the most revered protections under the first amendment, yet in our schools and universities it is being denied to students en masse. How can we expect the youth to grow into thoughtful, intelligent members of society when they have never been challenged? How will they be able to lead and innovate when they have always been spoon fed exactly what to say, think, and do? We are raising a generation of zombies not a generation of thinkers. We lack creativity and the ability to defend, challenge, or qualify an idea based on factual evidence or traditional values. WE CAN'T THINK. What can we expect, though, when our educational system is structured to enforce a social agenda instead of critical thinking skills?

Unfortunately, the adult population does not set a very good example in tolerating diversity of thought either. In fact, intellectual conformity is perhaps just as widespread in the workplace as it is in the public education system. Juan Williams found that out the hard way.

As a commentator on NPR, the government funded and decidedly left-wing National Public Radio service, Juan experienced firsthand the Left's unforgiving intolerance for those who didn't conform to their rigid beliefs. Though he had worked for NPR for years, Juan also picked up a weekly appearance on Fox News's Bill O'reilly program. He, a Democrat, and Mary-Katherine Ham, a conservative, enjoy a weekly segment all to themselves on the program. Fair and balanced, Juan served as the

First Principles for my First Election

voice for giving a Democratic perspective on the issues and Mary-Katherine argues from the conservative point of view. It was just another job.

To Juan's dismay, however, NPR fired their long loyal employee who had served them faithfully for over a decade out of sheer political intolerance. After making the following comments on Fox News, NPR took the initiative to fire Mr. Williams.

"I mean, look, Bill, I'm not a bigot. You know the kind of books I've written about the civil rights movement in this country. But when I get on the plane, I got to tell you, if I see people who are in Muslim garb and I think, you know, they are identifying themselves first and foremost as Muslims, I get worried. I get nervous."[15]

Ellen Weiss, Juan's boss, condemned the comments as bigoted and promptly sacked Williams. It's obvious though that this was only the straw that broke the camel's back. The facts show, as does Juan's own testimony, that his relationship with NPR was never quite smooth. NPR had furiously requested that he stop appearing on the O'reilly Factor years ago. When he refused, NPR requested Fox News not to identify him as a "NPR Political Analysts" any longer. That was in 2009 –a year before he was fired. Conclusion: liberals absolutely love free speech –for other

Intellectual Independence

liberals (and really only liberals that conform to their purist ideology).

The day after he was fired, Juan Williams published his opinion on the whole deal. He began by stating, "Yesterday, NPR fired me for telling the truth. The truth is that I worry when I am getting on an airplane and see people dressed in garb that identifies them first and foremost as Muslim. This is not a bigoted statement. It is a statement of my feelings, my fears after the terrorist attacks of 9/11 by radical Muslims."[16] That is an honest answer. (What did NPR want him to do, lie?) It is an emotion, however rational or irrational you deem it to be, and that feeling is common in post-9/11 America. Juan Williams went on to condemn this action by NPR, which was obviously politically motivated, and said:

"This is an outrageous violation of journalistic standards and ethics by management that has no use for a diversity of opinion, ideas, or diversity of staff (I was the only black male on the air). This is evidence of one party rule and one sided thinking at NPR that leads to enforced ideology, speech, and writing. It leads to people, especially journalists, to be sent to the gulag for raising the wrong questions and displaying an independence of thought."[17]

Mr. Williams was astonished when his own employers, his own friends turned on him for political reasons. He called the

First Principles for my First Election

entire debacle "a chilling assault on free speech." He then stated, "The critical importance of honest journalism and a free flowing, respectful national conversation needs to be had in our country. But it is being buried as collateral damage in a war whose battles include political correctness and ideological orthodoxy."

Juan is now the author of the new book *Muzzled: The Assault on Honest Debate.* It is important to reiterate that Juan Williams is a *Democrat*. His experience and free admission that the Left is supremely hypocritical and unjustly so, goes to show how obvious the problem of intellectual conformity is and how widely it permeates 21st century society. The fact remains that a certain group of political elites have an interest in silencing opposing voices. If they can't covert you in college, then they'll silence you as an adult.

Perhaps the favorite vehicle for silencing opposition, whether in school or at work, is the incorporation of political correctness into everyday life. If I had a nickel for every time I've kept my mouth shut because I was afraid of being politically incorrect, I could pay off the national debt! I'm sure most of you feel the same way. How many times can you think of when you didn't speak up because you might be called racist, or a homophobe, or intolerant? Well I've got news for you: you are not alone! It happens everyday with our friends, or our families, or our coworkers. There's no law that prevents us from exercising that free speech, that's why political correctness is so devastating

Intellectual Independence

to it. It is a self-imposed tyranny –one contrived by the Left and planted in your heart of hearts by subtle and deceptive societal pressure. It is another emotional ploy to confuse you into maintaining the status-quo, letting the truth go untold, and smothering your intellectual independence.

As dangerous as political correctness can be to the intellectual independence of a free society, physical confrontation in the form of heckling can be even more threatening. Heckling is the peaceful or violent disruption of a speaking engagement for the purposes of making a political statement. Its chief aim is to invoke the feeling of fear previously discussed in this chapter in both the speaker and the audience. Terror, however cruel, can be quite effective in preventing public deviance from a socially desired conformity and can do wonders to stifle diversity of thought.

I have witnessed this kind of heckling first hand. In November of 2011, I attended a Reagan Day Dinner hosted by the Heritage Foundation and co-sponsored by Linchpins of Liberty. The keynote speaker was former Secretary of State Donald Rumsfeld. After several minutes into his speech, a rather large lady stood up in the middle of the audience, pointed her finger squarely at the former Secretary, and yelled at the top of her lungs, "Donald Rumsfeld, you're a war criminal! You're a war criminal! You lied to the American people!" etcetera, etcetera. She was quickly

First Principles for my First Election

escorted out of the event by security as she wildly flailed her arms about and continued shouting her rude remarks.

Surprisingly, Secretary Rumsfeld kept his composure throughout the entire debacle –even smiling at the seemingly deranged woman. My first feeling was fear. Likewise, several of my friends from my high school's Young Conservatives club were visibly distressed. One girl told me that she didn't feel safe and asked if she could leave. I reassured her that everything was okay, but little did I know, there were more interlopers yet to show themselves later that night.

A few minutes later, another woman stood up in the crowd and shouted similar things. She seemed to resist her security escorts even more violently. Next, a bald man followed suit. By the end of the night, Secretary Rumsfeld's speech had been interrupted three or four times and those in the audience were utterly disturbed.

That was my first encounter with the Occupy movement which started the previous summer. These community agitators had infiltrated this political event in order to heckle a prominent guest speaker and a national hero in the war on terror. For all their supposed "open-mindedness," these leftists had no tolerance for a conservative speaker whatsoever and took time out of their personal lives to put on this childish charade. The occupiers also lied in order to get into the event. Claiming they were students, they signed up for the event at a discounted rate. Then, to their

Intellectual Independence

surprise, a local veteran offered to pay the entire cost of admission for the group, being under the impression that they were innocent teenagers who simply wanted to get engaged in the community. Afterward, the protestors showed a video to local news stations which they had taken on their phones during the incident. When interviewed, the agitators were drunk off their own cockiness and impropriety. They yelled hysterically as they cheered their victory of chaotic disruption. Apparently free speech doesn't apply to conservatives.

I remember vividly the series of emotions that my friends and I experienced that night. First was fear. Of course, that was the purpose of the Occupy hecklers. Obviously the agitators did not think that Rumsfeld would abandon his speech simply because of them. Their only goal was to induce fear and intimidation in the hearts of conservatives. To some extent it worked. However, another feeling quickly replaced our fear –anger and frustration. We became furiously mad at the Occupiers who rudely disrupted our otherwise wonderful event and frightened us with outlandishly bizarre behavior. We were mad that they would treat a distinguished guest in such a rude manner, and we were mad that all rules of free speech and civility seemed to be thrown out the window simply because we were conservatives. The power and force of the mob is truly disturbing, as I experienced firsthand. Ann Coulter's book *Demonic* is eerily reminiscent of this fact.

Apparently, the principle of conformity rules both the

First Principles for my First Election

world of school and the world of work. Disagree with your teacher? Suffer from a bad grade. Disagree with the collective wisdom (or what you perceive to be the latest fad) of the day? Suffer social ostracism. Deviate from your boss's rigid ideology? Get fired. Become a conservative public figure? Get heckled.

    The solution to the current state of affairs is to declare intellectual independence –independence from the machine, from the establishment, and from all the forces which have hindered us from fulfilling our potential and being the masters of our own destiny. The thoughts of the Spanish philosopher Santayana echo the exact motivations for declaring such independence from a culture of conformity, "The intellectual world of my time alienated me intellectually. It was a Babel of false principles and blind cravings, a zoological garden of the mind, and I had no desire to be one of the beasts."[18] The quest for intellectual independence is to bring order to the mind, leaving behind the false principles and blind cravings of the masses. It is to be transformed by the renewing of our mind, leaving behind the beast inside all of us and becoming truly human. It is a quest for self-discovery. To declare independence from the education establishment means to engage in a lifelong journey of self-education. The only way to be prepared for the onslaught from liberal academics and professors is to be firm in your convictions *before* you're confronted by them! In order to be firm in your

Intellectual Independence

convictions, however, you must take the initiative to reconnect with your first principles, with our nation's first principles.

So often, when I stumble upon a book by a great conservative thinker (or more often than not when I am directed to one by a friend or mentor), I catch myself thinking, *Why haven't I heard of this guy?* If you have read this far, you might be wondering the same thing by now. How come I have not heard of intellectual giants like Russell Kirk, or Orestes Brownson, Richard Weaver, (and later) Edmund Burke and C.S. Lewis? The simple fact that you have not heard their names should clue you into the fact that something is being kept from you –something valuable, something important. As I have come to experience these authors myself, I hope to pass on some of their most interesting ideas and teachings that offer a healthy and refreshing counter balance to the liberal propaganda we are bombarded with at school. There are great ideas and principles articulated by these conservative thinkers that are just waiting to be rediscovered. The power and potential of our generation rests in our inherent curiosity to pursue real truth and honest answers –answers that can only be found in books of our forefathers. For surely, "A *little* learning is a dangerous thing, Alexander Pope instructs us. Certainly it is unhealthy to remain lifelong a presumptuous sophomore, assertive that one has the answers to riddles which have

First Principles for my First Election

perplexed the good and wise since the age of Job and earlier (emphasis mine)."[19]

This means that our generation needs to catch up on our reading! We need to read the right books and rediscover our history and our heritage. This will take time and effort, but the only alternative is to lean on the propaganda of the establishment. Seriously, who wants to live in the dark once made aware of the perilous state of affairs? Who could reject truth when confronted with lies? Who could be good but let evil triumph? Only a coward.

Millennials have been taken advantage of and used. We need to fight back, not with guns or weapons, but with ideas. We need to fight back intellectually. Stand up to the lies, the deceit, and the biased corruption! Stand up! THINK! Don't conform into the image of what others force upon you. Be an individual. Think for yourself. Discover who you are. Believe in something.

It matters little to me whether you agree with me on specific political policies. It matters to me whether the thoughts, emotions, and ideas which you possess are genuine and individually produced. Do you believe what you say you believe? Can you *support* your belief with evidence or articulate it clearly? Or do you believe it because your parents, or teachers, or friends believe it? Furthermore, do you know why you believe it? Can you back up your position with facts,

Intellectual Independence

principles, and reflection on historical experience? Do you really have a full understanding of the issues or only a superficial understanding of partisan talking points? What are your principles?

Most people cannot answer these questions without a little ball of guilt forming in their guts. We all know it is our civic duty to be informed, but most of us (me included) have neglected this duty, either out of ignorance or apathy. Until recently, I was a partisan. I defended Republicans because they were Republicans. I supported conservative policies because they were conservative policies. It wasn't that my parents were conservative, or that I was influenced negligibly. I truly believed some of the policies I supported and others I just had a gut feeling which drew on plain ol' common sense or political intuition.

It wasn't until I began to self-educate that I began to *understand* my own positions. I discovered my principles. I read; I watched the news; I sought guides and mentors; I pursued Truth. Two years ago I read Russell Kirk's *The Roots of American Order* after being introduced to it by a mentor. Through this book I discovered the historical roots of our western, our American, order. I gained a great appreciation for moral order, political order, and historical perspective. Kirk articulated why I felt and believe the things I did. Most of my opinions were not reversed (though some were), but rather

First Principles for my First Election

strengthened. It helped me connect the dots between principle, policy, and historical experience. I discovered myself.

In the last year, I also read through the Bible. This was an attempt to challenge my faith. It worked. Though I will get into the specifics of exploring the order of the soul in the next chapter, it is important to mention that challenging your faith is a vital part of self-education in the quest for self-discovery. This is complete intellectual independence.

So I would encourage everyone to read, read, read! You can't rely on faulty information from others. Find out for yourself. Do not believe everything you read or hear. Do not believe me! Double check every fact and in the words of Jefferson, "question with boldness."

"Question with boldness even the existence of a God; because, if there be one, he must more approve of the homage of reason, than that of blind-folded fear..."[20]

Read. Self-educate. Question with boldness.

The next step in declaring your independence from the Machine requires more confrontation. At some point, this madness has to stop. The liberal monopoly on education cannot be allowed to continue unchecked as kids pass into adulthood without developing a rational thought process as an individual, not

Intellectual Independence

as a part of a collective, or as a decree handed down by a professor. Someone has to have the backbone to stand up to this nonsense. Speak out! Stop giving in to the machine. Stop sacrificing principles for grades. Stop sucking up to teachers that don't care about your intellectual development anyway. Stand up! Topple the establishment! We are the minority, for Pete's sake. We *are* the new counter culture.

We might have an uphill battle, and the establishment might wield more power, but we have the advantage of an energetic and rebellious youth, empowered with the sword of truth and a thirst for individual liberty. And needless to say, minorities have a history of winning uphill battles in America. Was it not the revolutionary Samuel Adams who declared,

"It does not require a majority to prevail, but rather an irate, tireless minority keen to set brush fires in people's minds."[21]

Finally, teach others. "Set brush fires in people's minds." Encourage one another in civic brotherhood, as Americans, to fulfill your patriotic duty to self-educate and to declare your independence from the machine. Teach one another what you have learned. Share books, share ideas, share thoughts, hopes, and dreams; but most of all, share your experiences. There is strength in numbers. Band together and do not be afraid to share the good

First Principles for my First Election

news. Bring others to independence by powerful force of truth. For the truth, and the truth alone, will set you free.

I chose the topic of "intellectual independence" for the first chapter to give you a glimpse into the direction of this book. Intellectual independence is a principle that has extreme value –especially for the youth, to whom it has been most deprived. In my opinion it should be the first commonplace principle from which Millennials of all ideological backgrounds can unite behind going forward into the 2012 election. Intellectual Independence.

We must declare it from the rooftops. With unmistakable clarity we must declare independence from the establishment, thereby unlocking the shackles of conformity and collectivism. We must declare our freedom of thought and freedom of speech from those who have used their authority to silence us. We must declare and decry the crimes against liberty and the perpetrators thereof. We must declare to the world our resolve to once again rise up and correct the wrongs of our parents and grandparents. We must declare to ourselves the need for self-education and self-discovery. We must declare in breath-taking unity our thirst for genuine, unbiased, unadulterated, TRUTH. We must declare our intellectual independence!

Principle #2

Moral Courage

As mentioned earlier, one in every four Millennials have declared themselves either atheist or agnostics.[a] This percentage, while not a majority, is astounding because it far surpasses that of the national average and it has more than doubled in only 20 years. Not surprisingly, this exponential rise of a-religious and sometimes anti-religious mentality directly correlates with the liberal takeover of education. Few other explanations have been offered.

Drawing from their inherent elitism, progressive professors preach that "religion is the opium of the masses" –a

---

[a] An atheist being one that denies the existence of God and creation altogether, and an agnostic being one who is skeptical of the existence of God, yet holding out the possibility of His existence.

First Principles for my First Election

phrase coined by the Soviet's own Lenin. According to this idea, religion is a drug that the mass of uneducated, foolish, and ignorant people use to make them feel better. It comprises of fairy tales for the youngsters, and threats of hell for mature. It develops a backwards way of thinking and promotes narrow-mindedness and intolerance. Unfortunately, Millennials have fallen for this hateful propaganda: hook, line, and sinker.

    What are the consequences of an ever-growing secular society? What are the consequences of rejecting our true spiritual heritage and pretending to be something that we are not? The only thing that can come of such phony irresponsibility is the destruction of the American Order and the deterioration of the cultural fabric that holds us together. Professors falsely preach that the civil society can be maintained by a secular populace. They naively assume that by instituting the right political system, government will be able to solve the nation's woes. Our government's past interventions in other countries is reflective of this "nation-building" mentality. However, there is much more to the creation and maintenance of civil society than merely transplanting a political system onto a foreign people and simply hoping that they understand and agree with our Western conceptions of liberty and toleration. It is quite possible that some cultures will never experience the profound

Moral Courage

order which has uniquely developed in the United States. Some sort of *moral order* is required for the preservation of liberty. How else can a people unite behind certain core principles and discern between right and wrong, liberty and tyranny? 20th century historian Russell Kirk sums it up nicely:

"All aspects of any civilization arise out of a people's religion: its politics, its economics, its arts, its sciences, even its simple crafts are the by-products of religious insights and a religious cult. For until human beings are tied together by some common faith, and share certain moral principles, they prey upon one another. In the common worship of the cult, a community forms. At the heart of every culture is a body of ethics, of distinctions between good and evil; and in the beginning, at least, those distinctions are founded upon the authority of revealed religion. Not until a people have come to share religious belief are they able to work together satisfactorily, or even to make sense of the world in which they find themselves. Thus all order –even the ideological order of modern totalistic states, professing atheism –could not have come into existence, had it not grown out of general belief in truths that are perceived by the moral imagination."[22]

The Fall of the Roman Republic is reminiscent of this fact. While maintaining a brilliant system of government –a

First Principles for my First Election

republic (which our own founding fathers would later remember), The Roman people failed to maintain a moral order. They deserted their faith and *pietas,* the virtue of civic duty. Kirk explains,

"The late Roman world, then, was a culture spiritually impoverished and disordered, lacking a common core belief. It has been called a dead world: a time in which the old Roman virtues had been lost by the mass of men, but in which the Christian virtues had not yet come to dominate. It was a world spiritually and intellectually bored. Mankind can endure anything but boredom. *Because men could not order their own despairing souls, the order of the commonwealth could not be saved.* (emphasis, mine)."[23]

The Roman Republic fell due to many reasons. Financial misdealing and military overexpansion are among the most sighted. Perhaps the straw that broke the camel's back however, was the lack of moral virtue. Corruption. Greed. Materialism. These challenges and temptations are the same which now face the American Republic as we have become richest of all nations. Already our financial status is quickly deteriorating (to be discussed later). Our president is overextending our military while denying them money. And religion has come over a wave of attacks, criticisms, and

Moral Courage

skepticism. Will Millennials have the moral courage to reverse the status-quo and the will to save our country?

The number one thing in the way of that dream is a wall erected by the powerful liberal machine. You have all heard of the wall which separates us –moral crusaders for change- from touching the hearts and minds of others. The wall which seems to have been taught to us from childhood. The mythical "wall of separation" between church and state.

This is the bastion of liberal orthodoxy in regards to preventing the establishment of moral order. It is an enormous wall and a formidable barrier to success. However, when closely examined, it is not a fortress but an illusion.

Nevertheless, progressives are quick to point out the obvious "separation of church and state" that we enjoy in America. This argument, despite its fallacies, as held up remarkable well in recent years and has even penetrated the courts. It is the argument responsible for eliminating any public displays of religion on state or federal property. It is also the argument which has cast discussions of faith far from the premises of the classroom (lest unknowing children be influenced by the horrible, hate-filled teachings of Christianity…). Even the Supreme Court has ruled that voluntary prayer in schools, led by a teacher, are unconstitutional and violate the "Establishment Clause" of the

First Principles for my First Election

Constitution which supposedly erects the infamous "wall of separation."[24]

Unfortunately there exist these pesky, little things called "facts." This is what the "Establishment Clause" of the first amendment actually says:

"Congress shall make no law respecting an establishment of religion, or prohibiting the free exercise thereof…"

Notice that nowhere do the words "separation of church and state" appear (Actually the only word present in that beloved phrase is the preposition "of"). Furthermore, a proper reading would yield the obvious conclusion that the first amendment only applies to the federal government anyway. Even if *voluntary* prayer in schools could *possibly* constitute as state establishment of religion, the first amendment explicitly states that *Congress* shall make no law respecting an establishment of religion. Technically, though the Supreme Court mistakenly ruled to the contrary, the 50 states have free reign in areas of religious toleration.[b]

---

[b] Recently the High Court has adopted the judicial philosophy of "incorporation." Through incorporation, restrictions found in the Constitution which once only applied to the federal government have been applied to state governments as well. Ironically, the first amendment specifically says that "*Congress* shall make no law…" Thus, however valid the idea of incorporation may be, it specifically contradicts the spirit of the first amendment.

Moral Courage

So, if the wall of separation is not in the Constitution, then where did it come from? The truth is that the wall of separation is not founded in any sort of legal or political theory. Rather, the phrase was stolen and savagely ripped from its proper context from a letter of Thomas Jefferson to the Danbury Baptist Association in 1802 (15 years after the ratification of the Constitution). The Danbury Baptists, a minority in Connecticut, were concerned that their state government did not properly recognize religious freedom as an inalienable right, but only as a privilege. They feared meddling by the state and persecution, and so wrote to the commander in chief for advice and assurance for the survival of religious liberty. President Jefferson wrote back, and though he did not address their concerns with their own state government, he reiterated that the Constitution specifically protected from intervention by the *federal* government, thus erecting a metaphorical wall of separation.[25]

An honest analysis shows that the first amendment (and the alluded wall of separation) was only directed at the federal government and was a measure to protect the church from the state, not the state from the church. Jefferson was assuring the Danbury Baptists that the federal government, at least under his watch, would protect religious minorities. In no way was he implying that the *government* should be rid of any and all religious influences.

First Principles for my First Election

A fact seldom mentioned is how much the government actually *supported* the church! Though the Founders had mixed opinions about the specific boundaries of church and state some such as Madison and even the "secular" Jefferson supported the idea that government should look, not negatively, not even neutrally, but *positively* upon religious activity. This came from the belief that "Of all the dispositions and habits which lead to political prosperity, religion and morality are indispensable supports" as articulated by our first president George Washington.[26] In other words, the activities of the church (maintaining the spiritual fiber of the nation, caring for the poor, and providing a place to worship the Almighty) were helpful and in fact necessary for the preservation of American society. Thus during the early Republic, the government had no problem with assisting churches financially –a claim far from that of the perpetrators of the separation myth. Just to underline this mainstream belief, let us look at some examples of how Thomas Jefferson –the "secularist"- supported the role of the church:

- Jefferson urged local governments to make land available specifically for Christian purposes
- Jefferson assured a Christian religious school that it would receive "the patronage of the government"

Moral Courage

- In an 1803 federal Indian treaty, Jefferson willingly agreed to provide $300 to "assist the said Kaskaskia tribe in the erection of a church" and to provide "annually for seven years $100 towards the support of a Catholic priest." He also signed three separate acts setting aside government lands for the sole use of religious groups and setting aside government lands so that Moravian missionaries might be assisted in "promoting Christianity."
- As mentioned earlier, when Washington D. C. became the national capital in 1800, Congress voted that the Capitol building would also serve as a church building. President Jefferson chose to attend church each Sunday at the Capitol and even provided the service with paid government musicians to assist in its worship. Jefferson also began similar Christian services in his own Executive Branch, both at the Treasury Building and at the War Office.[27]

What does this have to do with moral courage? –Everything!

The myth of the wall of separation is the epitome of liberal indoctrination and of intellectual, as well as moral deprivation. Under the false justification of "the wall" progressives have effectively stomped out the flame of the moral imagination in public schools. Daily prayer has been replaced by an annoying

First Principles for my First Election

and awkward "moment of silence" which no one participates in for fear of sideways glances and dirty looks form friends and teachers. Even *discussion* of religion, morality, or ethics is heresy. Violations of the sacred secularism can result in detention, low test grades, and social alienation.

Students are daily robbed of their religious liberty to freely express their own ideas about creation, morality, and God. It is one thing to rob an individual of his thought, of his intellectual independence. The obvious extension of that unfortunately, is to rob one of his moral imagination, which includes the natural inclination of man to ponder his existence and purpose in the world. Students who make any attempt to break outside the sacred box of secularism imposed upon them by the public school bureaucracy are severely punished. In a way, an analogy can be drawn between the operation of the uncompromising secularism of public education and the early, legalistic Catholic Church. Both hold their ideas to be sacred, and both have a terrible track record of toleration. The early Catholic Church is known for its uncompromising nature and severe punishment for those who questioned its teachings (if there is one thing the Left loves to teach, it is the shortcomings of organized religion). The great irony, however, is though religious leaders have progressed past burning people at the stake and handing down severe punishments for heretics (at least the Christians have), the secular Left imitates these

Moral Courage

legalistic and narrow-minded attitudes still today! While condemning the sacred and divine as narrow-minded and having a monopoly on truth, they themselves hold secularism to be sacred and absolute. Millennials feel the wrath of sacred secularism daily. It is a wonder students of faith are not yet martyrs.

In reality, the circles on the Left that are most guilty of this hypocritical intolerance are the militant environmentalist groups. Amongst the various environmental groups there is one common theme: radically religious dedication to the green movement. It really has become a religion, or more of a cult. Some on the fringe of the movement really do come across as Earth-worshiping, Mother-Earth-loving, people, right? There motives seem altruistic and good on the outside, but some groups have more resemblance to the darker and more intolerant aspects of a cult. I mentioned earlier, that the Left likes to point out the rampant intolerance of the Roman Catholic Church and its persecution of heretics at certain points in its long history. But do the same people so critical of the Church inform you of militant environmentalists who advocate the execution of those who do harm to Mother Earth?

Radical environmentalist group Alternet.org published an article that interviewed several leaders of the militant branch of the green-movement who did advocate such state-sponsored

First Principles for my First Election

killings. Activist Derrick Jensen said, "If it were up to me, all the people associated with the Gulf oil spill, which is murdering the Gulf, would be executed. That would be part of the function of a state."[28] Lierre Keith, and Aric McBay, who were also interviewed, discussed their book Green Deep Resistance which openly called for "direct attacks on infrastructure" and evil, capitalist, earth-destroying businesses. Now who seems more radical and intolerant –Christians, or environmentalists?

Before you answer that, look at a few more examples. Alternet is far from the only militant environmentalist group. In fact, there are organizations far worse and far more dangerous. The Earth Liberation Front (ELF) and Animal Liberation Front (ALF) specialize in violent acts against industry. Finding their origins in the radical and violent decades of the 1960's and 170's, these groups have been repeatedly put on the FBI's most wanted list. A 2009 press release by the FBI reported that, "Animal rights and environmental extremism pose a significant domestic terrorism threat. To date, extremists have been responsible for more than 1,800 criminal acts and more than $110 million in damages…"[29] These acts of eco-terrorism include arson and bombings of private property and public infrastructure. One of the most costly attacks included a massive arson in which seven separate fires caused $12 million in damage to three buildings and several chair lifts at a ski resort in Vail, Colorado in 1997. Of the

Moral Courage

event, ELF commented, "putting profits ahead of Colorado's wildlife will not be tolerated....We will be back if this greedy corporation continues to trespass into wild and unroaded [sic] areas." After set fire to a five story building in San Deigo, the organization put up a banner that read, "If you build it, we'll burn it."[30]

All this is not to say that anyone who is sympathetic to the green-movement is also sympathetic to these putrid acts of violence. I am not so naïve. I do think it is worth of pointing out however that the national media typically turns a blind eye to such acts of terror when committed on the Left, but when a crack-pot pastor even threatens to burn a Koran in a small Florida town it becomes not national, but world-wide news. Yet the media's blind eye ignores issues of greater importance. These examples must be made in order to show the blatant hypocrisy by the sacred secularists. Religion must be condemned as narrow-minded and uncompromising, but secularism's shortcomings should not be up for discussion. Their intolerance permeates all aspects of our culture and is obvious in all steps in life. Sacred secularism transcends the environmental extremism of ELF and other such organizations. It can even be found in the public school system, where students of faith are the defenseless minority and must submit under an oppressive system of fear.

Science classes are ground zero in the war for moral imagination against the secular intolerance of the Left. The

First Principles for my First Election

Theory of Evolution is forced down the throats of teens, defenseless against the power and authority of the teacher. It is advised not to bite the hand that feeds you. Likewise, students are slow to bite that hand that grades their tests. Under the threat of failure or disciplinary measures, students are forced to accept that the inherent beauty and genius of mankind and its superiority to all other creatures is merely coincidence, and a product of a disputed scientist's theory of natural selection.

There is no room for debate, discussion, or questions. It is science, we are told. (It is science just as Global Warming is science now, and just as Global Cooling was science in the 1970's.) Despite the number of scientists who reject the theory of evolution and even claim empirical evidence against it, students are withheld from any opposing view, let alone are they provided with opportunity for discussion. Some have advocated allowing teachers to present alternative theories of scientists, including theories of intelligent design (the idea that the universe was actually created, and created with definite order, and did not just pop into existence on its own accord). As of this writing two states –Louisiana and my home state of Tennessee- have taken action by passing laws that protect teachers who introduce different scientific theories on creationism and evolution.[31] This is a good first step toward academic freedom and intellectual independence for students, but only time will tell whether or not simple legislation will be enough to override the fear factor for teachers who dare to deviate from the established doctrine of the Left.

Opponents ignorantly throw accusations of wanting to teach "religion" in schools, thus violating the alleged "separation of church and state". This falsely categorizes the concept of intelligent design, which deals with scientific evidence and theories, not religion. In fact, it is quite narrow-minded and insensitive to suggest or even imply that intelligent design would only serve the purposes of the evil, theocratic Christians. Obviously all students of faith, regardless of religion, would be interested in hearing alternative scientific views on the subject of creation. According to the Pew Research Center who surveyed scientists who were members of the American Association for the Advancement of Science, only 40% of scientists do not believe in God. 60% believe in either a God or some other higher power. While the number of believing scientists is significantly lower than the general public (which estimates show about 90% of who believe in some sort of deity), it is obvious that there is a diversity of thought on the issue among the nation's brightest.[32] Evolution itself has various support or lack thereof among the scientific community. Some scientists only confirm the existence of micro-evolution, some macro-evolution, and some neither. One fact remains certain however: The absolute intolerance of the evolutionists also

First Principles for my First Election

sheds light on the lack of confidence in their argument. If evolution is the unmistakable, legitimate truth, then what have they to fear of introducing other scientific theories? Will not truth set you free?

Historian Paul Johnson wrote in his book *Modern Times (The World From The Twenties To The Nineties),* that even Einstein who made ground breaking discoveries as to the operation of our universe, believed in a God and moral absolutes. Ironically, and to his dismay, his theory of relatively was incorrectly used to "prove" *moral* relativism. Johnson writes,

"No one was more distressed than Einstein by this public misapprehension. He was bewildered by the relentless publicity and error which his work seemed to promote. He wrote to his colleague Max born on 9 September 1920: 'Like the man in the fairy-tale who turned everything he touched into gold, so with me everything turns into a fuss in the newspapers.' Einstein was not a practicing Jew, but he acknowledged a God. He believed passionately in absolute standards of right and wrong.

He lived to see moral relativism, to him a disease, become a social pandemic, just as he lived to see his fatal equation bring into existence nuclear warfare. There were times, he said at the end of his life, when he wished he had been a simple

Moral Courage

watchmaker.

The public response to relativity was one of the principal formative influences on the course of twentieth-century history. It formed a knife, inadvertently wielded by its author, to help cut society adrift from its traditional moorings in the faith and morals of Judeo-Christian culture."[33]

Apparently, given the evidence, the Left just likes to pick in choose which scientists to teach and when. Facts fade away into irrelevancy.

Yet religious liberty is assaulted not only in science classrooms. In English students are taught to avoid at all costs the use of moral argument in their writing. Essays should be entirely secular and their rhetorical appeal should not depend upon morality or ethics. Millennials are taught that moral argument is bad and irrelevant. One cannot argue on the merit of ethics, because in reality, no real Truth exists. For this reason I have personally had teachers tell me that I couldn't write a paper on topics like abortion or capital punishment because "they're just too religious."

The alleged "wall of separation" permeates throughout the classrooms of public schools, bleeding into all areas such as Science and English, but most of all History. Secular revisionists have rewritten history textbooks which now amount to appraisal of how the early Republic so enshrined

First Principles for my First Election

"secularism" in society. While revisionists are quick to denounce the Founders as an elitist, planter class group of old, white, men, they simultaneously praise their supposed "secularism." The suggestion that the Founders were anything but a devoutly religious and spiritual group of individuals would be an outright lie.

Crack open any modern history textbook, and one will find that the only Founders whose spiritual lives are discussed in detail are that of the two or three least spiritual –Thomas Jefferson, Ben Franklin, and sometimes Thomas Paine - conveniently neglecting to mention the more than 200 other Founding Fathers, 55 of whom attended the Constitutional Convention. Nearly all were Christians, and those with notable historical roles include George Washington, John Adams, James Madison, Patrick Henry, Alexander Hamilton, etc.

Moral Courage

> Other Religious Founding Fathers:
>
> - Charles Pinckney and John Langdon—founders of the American Bible Society
> - James McHenry—founder of the Baltimore Bible Society
> - Rufus King—helped found a Bible society for Anglicans
> - Abraham Baldwin—a chaplain in the Revolution and considered the youngest theologian in America
> - Roger Sherman, William Samuel Johnson, John Dickinson, and Jacob Broom—also theological writers
> - James Wilson and William Patterson—placed on the Supreme Court by President George Washington, they had prayer over juries in the U. S. Supreme Court room

Even so, the least religious of the Founders, who revisionists rashly brand as "Deists," are often mischaracterized. Thomas Jefferson, who supposedly supported a "wall of separation," in fact allowed the U.S. Capital building to be used as a church every Sunday during his presidency. At the time, it was the largest church in the United States. Jefferson, his successor Madison, and many other presidents and members of Congress attended Church regularly at the Capital establishing a precedent that would last well after the Civil War. (this originating from a supposed

First Principles for my First Election

opponent to the integration of religious influence into government.

Benjamin Franklin, another whom the Left quickly point to as a rational voice of secular enlightenment, was not as hostile to religion as we are led to believe. Not only was Franklin widely supportive of Christian activities, but when his friend Thomas Paine published his book *Age of Reason*, Franklin wrote Paine a harsh letter condemning his denunciation of the inherent

> Other things to consider:
>
> "Franklin proposed a Biblical inscription for the Seal of the United States; that he chose a New Testament verse for the motto of the Philadelphia Hospital; that he was one of the chief voices behind the establishment of a paid chaplain in Congress; and that when in 1787 when Franklin helped found the college which bore his name, it was dedicated as 'a nursery of religion and learning' built 'on Christ, the Corner-Stone.'"

goodness of Christianity and the virtue it encourages in society. Franklin argues that religion can only build up society and it should not be treated as some vile threat to be attacked and sent to the slaughter. Also, neglected by revisionist historians is the following quote from Benjamin Franklin regarding his personal religious beliefs: "Here is my creed: I believe in one God, the Creator of the universe. That he governs it by his providence. That he ought to be worshipped. That the most acceptable service we render to him is in doing good to his other children. That the soul

Moral Courage

of man is immortal, and will be treated with justice in another life respecting its conduct in this. These I take to be the fundamental points in all sound religion."[34] This man does not sound secular to me.

In fact, some suggest that Benjamin Franklin turned to Christianity outright towards the end of his life and abandoned his deistic views of an impersonal and non-interventionist God. At a point of great distress and uncertainty in the halls of Philadelphia during the Constitutional Convention, 80 year old Benjamin Franklin stood up –the oldest of the members in attendance and offered a piece of elderly advice, as well as a call for prayer:

"And have we forgotten that powerful Friend? Or do we imagine that we no longer need His assistance? I have lived, sir, a long time and the longer I live the more convincing proofs I see of this truth: that *God governs in the affairs of men*. And if a sparrow cannot fall to the ground without his notice, is it probable that an empire can rise without His aid? We have been assured, sir, in the sacred writings that 'except the Lord build the house, they labor in vain that build it.' I firmly believe this and I also believe that without His concurring aid, we shall succeed in this political building no better than the builders of Babel [emphasis, mine]."[35]

Even Thomas Paine, by far the least religious of the Founders, can be found to be at least spiritual in that he expressed

First Principles for my First Election

belief that man was created by a Supreme Being. In fact he even supported the teaching of creationism in schools: "It has been the error of schools to teach astronomy, and all the other sciences and subjects of natural philosophy, as accomplishments only; whereas they should be taught theologically, or with reference to the Being who is the Author of them: for all the principles of science are of divine origin. Man cannot make, or invent, or contrive principles; he can only discover them, and he ought to look through the discovery to the Author."[36]

Why are the boring historical facts of yesteryear relevant to Millennials? What do they have to do with moral courage?

The first step of recovering our generation's moral courage is *knowledge* –the knowledge that we have been lied to about our spiritual heritage. Our Founding Fathers were adamant about their faith and convicted of certain moral principles, largely found in Christian scripture. Those moral principles are what carried our nation thus far, providing the young Republic with virtuous leaders and a virtuous people to march the banner of liberty farther in two centuries than any other nation has done in the course of human history.[c] Moral courage begins with this knowledge.

---

[c] A book called *The 5,000 Year Leap* details this fact and discusses the specific principles which made America great. The title symbolizes the powerful impact that republican liberty had in a mere two centuries, compared to the generically

Moral Courage

With confidence in this newfound knowledge, we can have the moral courage to stand up for our beliefs. Religious liberty does not go away when we enter the doors of a public school. In the words of Thomas Jefferson, religious liberty is an "inalienable right" by which we were "endowed by our Creator." Millennials need to stand up for that right. Do not be silenced from evangelizing or spreading the Gospel. If you are not a Christian, do not be silenced or fearful to engage in religious conversation with your peers or to question the anti-religious actions of the establishment. If you are neither Christian, nor religious at all, won't you too stand up for your neighbor's right to freely express himself?

Again, these actions take courage. But what does moral courage look like? It means having the audacity to, dare I say it, bring a Bible to school! It means starting a study group with those of the same faith (whether Christian, Jewish, Hindu, etc.) It means questioning your teachers and professors on scientific "facts," or simply requesting the permission for teachers to teach alternative scientific theories. It means exploring for yourself your meaning and purpose in the world. It means not having to look over your shoulder before sharing your faith with another. It means not succumbing to political correctness. This kind of moral courage can only come from a conviction that America is genuinely a

---

slow march of human progress which is either subverted or reversed by the forces of tyranny.

First Principles for my First Election

religious nation (and historically, a Christian nation). Moral courage comes from the knowledge that religion has done nothing but bolster America's dominance in the world.

The Founding Fathers are not to be rebelled against. They were wise and noble men, designers of the grandest experiment, and securers of the blessings of liberty of which we all, even to this day, benefit grandly. But let us not limit our admirers to those men alone, but to American society as a whole. Generations before us built this nation –this empire of liberty- on the morals and values that all men are created equal under God and that they all have the right to seek and fulfill His will as they see fit. But more importantly, they knew that the worldly success they obtained was a direct result of their faith in something more powerful than themselves. From the very beginning, even during the trying times of the Revolution when hope was scarce, Americans still had "firm reliance on the protection from Divine Providence" as so pledged in their Declaration of Independence. Of this we can be confident: that by exhibiting moral courage we will not turn up empty-handed. If moral courage has brought our nation thus far, it can surely bring us further.

To contrast the direction of the sacred secularism of the Left and the religious fervency of the Founders, let us read the words of George Washington which he spoke in his first Inaugural address:

Moral Courage

"The preservation of the sacred fire of liberty, and the destiny of the republican model of government, are justly considered as deeply, perhaps as finally staked, on the experiment entrusted to the hands of the American people."[37]

Washington held that liberty was the sacred fire that kept the nation's spirit alive and in fact was deeply tied to the preservation of the Republic. The modern Left, however, holds some abstract idea of sacred secularism –the religion of faithlessness and intolerance- to be that divine keystone. If the keystone of Christ is ever replaced with this new keystone of man, our Republic will surely crumble.

If we are confident in our history, we must also be confident in our faith. It is necessary not only for Millennials to have the moral courage to stand up for their beliefs at school, but also to have the courage to apply the beliefs and convictions to personal life in the real world. Before we can even to begin applying the principle of moral courage, we must first become self-aware about our faith.

Most people are uncomfortable with religion. They go to church (synagogue, mosque, etc.) because their parents go, or because they have always done it; it is a routine. Others go because it makes them feel good. Some know that they should be there, but they do not want to be. And still others are perfectly complacent to stay at home and sleep in on Sunday mornings.

First Principles for my First Election

The fact is that most people have a very shallow understanding of their own religion or even about their beliefs in God in general. It is rare, and I think you would agree, to stumble upon someone who can perfectly articulate their theological beliefs and convictions, giving reasonable and sufficient evidence for them. Yet the apostle Peter commanded, "always be ready to make a defense to everyone who asks you to give an account for the hope that is in you (I Peter 3:15)."

Now, before you slam this book down in disgust for my rampant Bible-thumping, I should point out that I think this applies to all people of faith. (Obviously, I can only speak from my personal experiences.) Should not everyone attain that level of understanding about their faith? Is your relationship with God not the most important idea to consider? And if it is, shouldn't we be take responsibility to research, analyze, and discuss our beliefs about that relationship? I think so. But make no mistake; that level of in depth study requires both diligence and courage.

It is not easy to put yourself in a situation that challenges your long-held beliefs. It is not easy to "question with boldness" ideas of such magnitude and great importance. In fact, it is much simpler and less stressful to sit back and push away any thoughts or ideas about God or your spiritual responsibilities, meanwhile calling anyone who dares bring up the topic a radical, bigoted evangelist who cannot accept differences of opinion. That is the problem: people are afraid to even *have* an opinion. They could be

Moral Courage

wrong! And thus we have created the wonderful little label "agnostic" –for the individual who either doesn't care about his relationship with God, or who is too afraid to make a commitment.

Our generation cannot be the one to let the torch of the moral imagination burn out before it is passed along to the next generation of fellow Americans. We cannot succumb to the evils of moral deficiency, or worse, ambivalence. We need to set a new trend –a counter culture- in the quest to revive America's noble character and breathe fresh air into the flame of liberty, lest we allow secularism to extinguish our passion for justice and pursuit of eternal truth and our empire of liberty earn itself a miserable death akin to our Roman heritage.

Whatever your religion, be confident of it. Be sure of it. Believe it and practice it in your daily life. Know God and love him with all of your heart, with all of your mind, with all of your soul, and with all of your strength. I challenge you to challenge yourself. Whether you are a religious person, an agnostic, or even an atheist, ask the tough questions: Why am I here? Does my life have purpose? Do I have a creator? What is his relationship to me? Does he love me? What do I believe about life after death?

I could have just as easily entitled this chapter "Moral Curiosity." Curiosity is what drives conservative thought, and it is the void of curiosity that distinguishes the Left from its conservative counterpart. The Left hates curiosity. Curiosity –

First Principles for my First Election

whether intellectual or moral- gives the potential for individuality and ultimately the discovery of genuine Truth. The Left is primarily concerned with the destruction of the individual and his subservience to the state, or the "general will" of the people as Rousseau would say. Intellectual curiosity would not fulfill that purpose, because it allows one to question authority, the basis for all liberal strength. Likewise, moral curiosity would only liberate man from his sinful nature and give him a hope and faith in the Eternal. Man cannot have two masters, both God and the State, thus moral curiosity poses problems as well.

Conservatives hold however, that moral curiosity is the foundation of a free-thinking, civil society and is paramount for its survival. Conservatives urge people to "question with boldness" all things, and not to submit blindly to ideological doctrines or partisan talking points. The same goes with

> "Regeneration, literacy or material, is possible only when the causes of an affliction have been properly apprehended. People who hope for renewed vigor in English and American letters need, then, to ascertain just how far the present apparent lassitude in the world of literature really is the product of social boredom, and what are the conditions that have brought such boredom into being… Literature thrives in an age of variety; it sickens in a time of uniformity. It seems to me that we have been working with the perverse will to reduce our civilization to an equalitarian uniformity." –Russell Kirk ("English Letters in the Age of Boredom," *Shenandoah* 7 (Spring, 1956): 11-12.)

Moral Courage

the quest for spiritual Truth. Conservatives believe that curiosity, questions, debates, and books are the key to unlocking the transcendent purpose of our lives.

The first step in your spiritual renewal is to get back to the basics. READ your holy text. In my personal efforts to become firmer in my faith, I made it my New Year's resolution last year to read through the entire Bible. I did it. It was difficult and challenging. At times I wanted to give up and other times I could not find the motivation to continue reading. However, with the encouragement from both my brother and my grandmother (both of whom also read through the whole Bible with me), and through diligent prayer and perseverance, I finished –one year later.

> "I am sure that most of you, at some stage of life, have read or have had read to you C.S. Lewis' charming series of parables about the battle of life, which he published under the general title of The Chronicles of Narnia. No children's books in this century have been more influential than the Lewis volumes, which is a reason for us to be hopeful about the twenty-first century." – Russell Kirk, 1986 Commencement Address at La Lumiere School

I also studied the book *Mere Christianity* by C.S. Lewis. If you are like me, you probably thought that C.S. Lewis was only famous for *The Chronicles of Narnia*. Upon further investigation, I found that not only were *The Chronicles of Narnia* a series of Biblical parables, but that Lewis was responsible for dozens of non-fiction pieces of theological

First Principles for my First Election

literature. In fact, I found that C.S. Lewis is commonly recognized as one of the greatest Christian thinkers of the 20th century! I am only now beginning to discover this man's ingenious works. *Mere Christianity* was a wonderful read. It was a great supplement to my Biblical understanding and it provided an alternate voice and a unique style of expression of the Gospels. I recommend it to anyone one who seeks to learn more about the Christian Faith, whether you are a believer or not. I would also recommend reading Lewis's *Miracles*, and *The Screwtape Letters* in order to challenge your moral imagination.

In my quest for spiritual growth, I also found myself enchanted by Rick Warren's book *The Purpose Driven Life*. In a time where most people, even people of faith, cannot articulate or even identify their purpose in life, this book gave me a renewed sense of optimism and direction as I seek to answer that question for myself. *The Purpose Driven Life* is meant to be read in 40 days, a chapter a day, to allow for the information to sink in. This breakdown makes it very manageable practically speaking. The other, and perhaps more significant reason for the 40 day breakdown, is the spiritual significance of a 40-day journey (as demonstrated repeatedly in the Bible by Jesus' 40 day fasting in the wilderness, Noah's 40 days of rain, Moses' 40 days on Mt. Sinai, the disciples 40 days of empowerment after the resurrection, etc.) This is a great outlet for your moral curiosity to do some exploring –especially if you are among the unfortunate

Moral Courage

souls who struggles daily with depression and a lack of enthusiasm for life. Warren's book changed my life, and I know it can change yours.

I do not tell you this to brag (but if I boast in anything, I will boast in the Lord!). I tell you this because of how much it meant to me. Reading through the Bible forced me to take a detour on my gentle, routine, peaceful walk with God. The detour was more of a hike. It was rugged, long, and at times confusing. However, as when one finishes a hike, a feeling of accomplishment and appreciation comes. A feeling of confidence and self-worth reward one's efforts. It brings health; in this case spiritual health. I was forced to delve beyond the traditional and favorite stories of Noah's ark, the parting of the Red Sea, the birth of Jesus, the acts of the early apostles, etc. I read of all those things, of course, but I also read the history of the Ancient Israelites. I read the oracles of the prophets who foresaw both the fall of God's chosen people and their eventual redemption through the Messiah. I read about Jesus' teachings of radical discipleship and unconditional love for both friends and enemies. I read the God-breathed epistles of the New Testament. I grew in my faith, all the while challenging myself to question things about my religion which I had never thought to question.

> "God does not despise the intellect which he created." –D. Deaton

This is what it means to apply moral courage to your own spiritual life. Break out of your routine. Do things that make you

First Principles for my First Election

uncomfortable. Do your research! I assure you that you will not conclude your studies empty-hearted. The Truth will either show you the error of your ways or confirm your deepest convictions; either way you win. You just have to have the courage to do it.

Do not misunderstand; Spiritual growth is a lifelong process. Reading once through your holy text is not enough. Moral courage means a lifelong application of a thirst for knowledge and understanding about your existence in the universe. It means finding your purpose in life and training yourself to articulate that purpose so that others may come to know the hope that you have, so that they too can be saved from a living a life without meaning.

How can civilization thrive when man finds no purpose in life? Put politics aside for the moment. What are the effects on society if man is taught, and accepts, that his life amounts to nothing more

> "Of all the dispositions and habits which lead to political prosperity, religion and morality are indispensable supports. In vain would that man claim the tribute of patriotism, who should labor to subvert these great pillars of human happiness, these firmest props of the duties of men and citizens…Let it simply be asked, where is the security for property, for reputation, for life, if the sense of religious obligation desert the oaths which are the instruments of investigation in courts of justice? And let us with caution indulge the supposition that morality can be maintained without religion. Whatever may be conceded to the influence of refined education…reason and experience both forbid us to expect that national morality can prevail in exclusion of religious principle." –George Washington

Moral Courage

than that of a rock, or a toad, or a bird? To what is man reduced? Is he not but an animal? A creature? A thing to be tamed? What law, legal or moral, can bind his actions from destruction?

This is what it means to have moral courage: to answer these questions without fear of consequence. It means to weigh the ramifications of what God means to you and what effect his influence has on society. This is not a political principle, but a moral one. All great leaders, regardless of faith have understood that only a religious people, a moral people, can uphold the civil society.

Once I asked my preacher for the greatest advice he could give to young people. He said, "Be right. Be nice. Be Fearless." First be right. Find out what you believe. Do your research and be bold in your convictions. Practice your faith to the fullest extent and learn to love God with all your heart, mind, and soul. Next be nice. Make sure not to be too intrusive when discussing matters of religion with others. Always have a kind and gentle spirit that reflects your love of God and his care for his children. And last, but not least, be fearless. Never be afraid to share the good news or smother your moral spirit. Let your light shine and engage others in the exchange of ideas. Set your moral imagination free!

So far we have defined the principle of moral courage and have suggested how it might be applied in both the realm of education as well as our personal lives. We have also explored, philosophically, why a lack of moral courage can be detrimental

First Principles for my First Election

to the strength of a nation. Now I want to discuss how this principle can apply to our community as a whole, and *specifically* why and how our generation can start a new precedent.

The strength of the Republic depends upon the moral fortitude of the citizenry. That strength is best embodied in our families, our personal relationships, and our spirit of community. Unfortunately, all three of those social institutions are

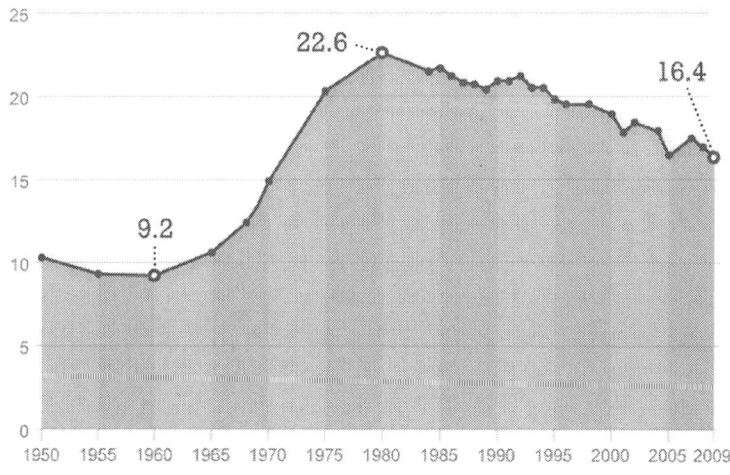

Note: Data after 1997 exclude multiple states.

deteriorating. Our generation is one of broken families, our relationships are phony, and our sense of spirit of community is dampened by self-interest and apathy. These three areas of social life are really the nuts and bolts of the larger, national moral deficiency, which Kirk asserts will have disastrous consequences. The Millennials are a generation of broken families. In 1960 the divorce rate was only 9%. With the surge of the sexual revolution, that number more than doubled in just two decades to 23%. Though the divorce rate has been steadily declining (it is now

Moral Courage

about 16%), it remains relatively high.[38] More important, though, is the fact that the divorce rate is largely dropping because less people are getting married in the first place. Only 56% of men and 53% of women are married. That is only half of the population! Again, that number results largely from the radical social changes from the sixties prior to which, the percentage of married adults hovered around 65 or 70%.[39]

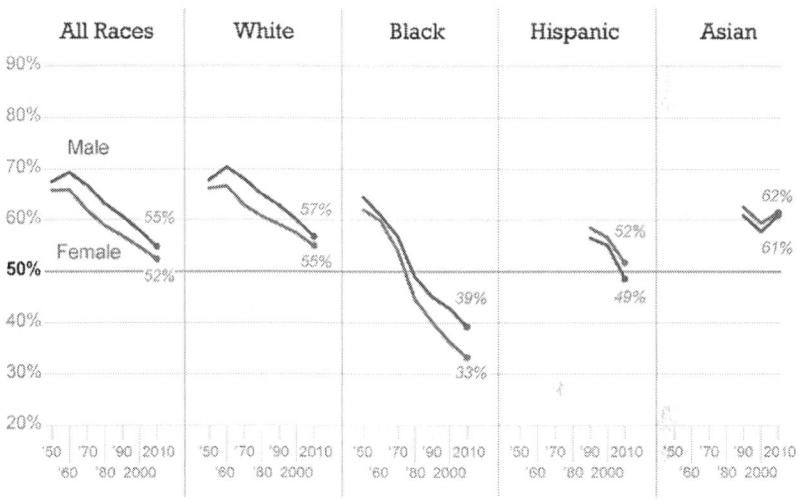

Note: Figures for 1950 and 1960 are for individuals age 14 and older.

The significance of these startling numbers however do not have anything to do with concern about the marital status of adults per se, but rather the detrimental sociological effects of those failed relationships on America's youth. 41% of children are born out of wedlock in America to struggling single mothers. This alarming percentage of the population is statistically prone to "host of hindrances to social mobility including emotional and behavioral problems, poor academic performance, and an increased risk of criminal activity." Children raised in single-parent households also have a higher susceptibility to a life of poverty.[40]

Does this mean that there is no love in a single-parent home, or that every child raised in such a home will end up on the streets? No! In fact, one of my best friends lives under the care of a single mother who I've met personally and can attest to her brilliant job at raising four kids. John Adams said that facts were "stubborn things," and stubborn as they are, statistics prove that children raised in a traditional home fair much better in society once they become independent. It is assumed that the loving care of a mother and the strong guidance and discipline of a father, along with their combined financial support add to a much healthier and stable environment for child-rearing –and thus a stronger society at large.

Here is yet another example of how our generation –the Millennials- has a unique opportunity to correct the wrongs of our parents. Really we have no legitimate reason to launch ourselves into the radical social movement of the secular progressives. The hippie movement is all but dead, and all that remains is a generation of morally confused adolescents and young adults (us), and the stubborn facts and figures that reveal the obvious failure of that movement.

I challenge you to set a new precedent: to resurrect the integrity of the family. You owe it to yourself. You owe it to your

Moral Courage

kids. And you owe it to your nation. Be better than your parents. Succeed where they failed. Get right what they got wrong. Have the moral courage to swim against the current that drags you toward impulsive immorality and radical individualism and away from moral sanity and family stability.

Another area where we have a responsibility to practice what we preach is in our personal relationships and our communities. It means nothing to find spiritual meaning or purpose, if you cannot apply your newfound moral principles to your life and be salt and light for others. If our generation could collectively make a conscience effort to forge stronger and more dynamic relationships, we could drastically improve the condition of the Republic. Get to know people for who they are, care for them. Love your neighbor as yourself. If people would do these simple things, it would solve a host of the world's problems, even without troubles of partisan politics.

And finally, be charitable. Have the moral courage to support your community through local churches or private charities. Put your faith in *these* institutions –the ones which we can really get involved with on a local level and monitor the activities thereof. Charity at its most basic is giving aid of some sort, be it love, compassion, or financial support, to someone in need. That role should be properly reserved to the aforementioned social institutions of society, not the government. A common misunderstanding by secular progressives of the more

First Principles for my First Election

conservative and religious segments of the population, is that those conservatives do not care about the poor or misfortunate. This could not be further from the truth! On principle, I believe it is every individual's responsibility to aid the poor who are powerless to lift themselves out of poverty –to help those who can't help themselves. This principle largely comes to me through my religious studies, and so too with other people of faith. But let emphasize one word: it is the *individual's* responsibility. I do not believe that society, or government owes anyone anything. Government exists only to secure certain natural liberties collectively, that which we can not well protect individually. However, republican government is not designed to be a nanny-state that supplies our every want and need. This is another reason why a Republic requires a more and virtuous people, so that they might fill that void of poverty and helplessness, instilling in their fellow man hope in a better future in this life and the next.

While pressing issues such as the health of the economy (or lack thereof), national security, illegal immigration, and others, tend to get most of the spotlight in the modern political arena, we must not forget that society cannot function without some basis of moral stability. The sacred social institutions of the church, the family, and community require protection in this present age of radical secularism. These moral institutions have little to do with politics, but they have everything to do

Moral Courage

with ourselves. The protection required to keep and sustain these institutions depend upon the degree of moral courage exhibited by every individual of the rising generation. The status-quo is unacceptable. A spiritually dull citizenry, raised in broken homes, who lack a sense of charity and goodwill toward their neighbors, is no recipe for a successful nation.

To reverse those trends requires moral courage. It requires the moral courage to pursue self-discovery in relation to one's purpose and place in the universe. It requires the moral courage to find one's own set of principles and values and it requires one to apply those values to his daily walk of life. It means raising a loving and healthy family, it means making meaningful relationships, and it means giving back to the community. Ultimately, no political platform or government policy can bring about this change. It is we the people, in particular we the Millennials, to resurrect the burning passion of our moral imagination and set free our moral curiosity.

Though I have already mentioned the concept of the "moral imagination" in conjunction with the virtues of moral courage and curiosity, I think it deserves a more thorough analysis, since it is so vital to the goals outlined above. Truly, courage and curiosity, in themselves, are useless without a fiery and bold imagination.

Moral imagination is a termed coined by the British statesman Edmund Burke in the 1700s. It is the idea that society

First Principles for my First Election

consists of more than mere individuals –more than isolated economic units in a grand market who strive toward material gain. Rather, it is the idea of community, fellowship, and a spiritual unity that unites the living and the dead. One who has "moral imagination" sees that the purpose of life consists of more than just getting rich quick, starting a family, and buying a house.

Moral imagination perceives a true happiness greater than what most consider the "American dream." It finds strength in relationships, in family, in tradition. It thrives in the context of religious devotion and a society free of government interference and social planning. It is the capability of an individual to find his place in the realm of a divine existence and to pursue his dreams in accordance to his Maker's will. To have moral imagination is to understand that *true* freedom is found in obedience to God.

This is where Millennials fall short in the war of ideas. Most Millennials probably find that they agree with the points I have outlined above, but they are woefully inadequate, or downright fearful, to communicate them articulately to a society hostile to the true freedom which the moral imagination seeks to restore. This is also where our libertarian friends go seriously wrong.

Liberals and libertarians alike fail to understand that society consists of so much more than individuals born with abstract "rights" and liberties which they claim are supremely superior to restraint by law. They view all people as mere individuals –as mere economic units, completely divorced from the context of family and community. They seem to think that their decisions only affect themselves. Conservatives understand that society does not function as a collection of individuals but as a complex and intricate body with varying and sometimes contradictory interests. For this reason, liberty must be under the law. It can be restrained and indeed it must be strained by government under certain circumstances. As Kirk writes,

"Men are never in a state of *total* independence of each other. It is not the condition of our nature; nor is it conceivable how any man can pursue a considerable course of action without its having some effect upon others; or of course, without producing some degree of responsibility for his conduct."[41]

It is extremely important for Millennials to rediscover this type of moral imagination (even if it may at first seem foreign to our modern minds) if we are to stand any chance at defending our customs and traditions articulately. Whether it's with the issue of gay marriage or drug legalization or any other liberal concoction, we have to learn to make the *moral* argument that one does not have a "right" to trample on the true rights of others. We do not have the right, as Kirk says, "to imperil the happiness of posterity by impudently tinkering with the heritage of humanity."[42] There are indeed unintended consequences to our moral choices that

First Principles for my First Election

affect other people. It is ludicrous for the state to ignore that fact under the cliché of the mythical "wall of separation" between church and state, which I discussed earlier.

We must learn how to articulate that conservatism is more than matters of dollars and cents. We have to stand for something more than tax breaks and spending cuts. We have to conserve something more than the path to prosperity. As Kirk so eloquently states,

"When the aim of life is to imitate the rich, and "opportunity" is made generally available, general discouragement is the consequence. No paradox, this: the average man, formerly content in his special craft or his old simplicities, is hopelessly out of the running in the race for wealth, and exhausts himself very early, and lingers on only in boredom."[43]

When all men desperately seek wealth, even at the assistance of the government, no one wins. Mediocrity reigns. Intellectual and moral curiosity dies. Think: the government gives everyone the opportunity to go to college so everyone can get rich. Now everyone goes to college and no one gets rich.

Luckily, there's more to life than getting rich. Yes, we must continue to defend private property and the free market against government intrusion and social leveling; but fiscal conservatism can't become its own end. If we want to win at the

Moral Courage

ballot box and if we want to succeed in restoring our nation, we must resurrect our moral imagination and understand what truly makes life worth the living.

This must be done on a cultural level; it cannot be achieved through any theocratic "political Christianity." Spiritual and moral regeneration must come through a change in culture – an inward change not an outward one. "Change we can believe in" will not come from government, but from an inward ordering of the soul. That is the essence of the true conservative mind and it must be the chief aim of all Millennials.

Imagination. Curiosity. Courage.

Principle #3

Entrepreneurship

Imagine: The year is 1879. On a cold winter night, somewhere in the parts of Menlo Park, New Jersey a large room filled with dozens of anxious men rushing around in a fantastic state of excitement, ecstatic about an invention that would revolutionize western culture. I don't know how it felt to be in the laboratory when Thomas Edison first invented the high-resistant incandescent light bulb, but I imagine the feeling was awe-inspiring. After at least three thousand trial and error attempts at finding a suitable filament material that could be used in electric lighting, this man finally made that discovery, and by 1880 Edison had brought to the marketplace a 16-watt bulb with the capacity of 1500 hours.[44] It revolutionized modern culture -both in the home and at the workplace. There rest, as they say, is history.

First Principles for my First Election

This one man's passion, his intellect, and his sheer spirit of determination and perseverance changed the world. Using his skills, his resources, and his brain, he invented a marketable item that benefited both him and society. We call this entrepreneurship. The natural successor to self-reliance, the power of the human mind to invent, create, and discover –entrepreneurship- is the very spirit that made America.

Unfortunately, that entrepreneurial spirit is being crushed under the colossal weight of government regulation. The same government that provided those opportunities and free markets under which the light bulb emerged, is the same government that is legally banning the incandescent light bulb today. And that is not a joke. The Energy Independence and Security Act of 2007 put into law a regulation that would 'phase out' the production of incandescent light bulbs in the U.S by introducing new energy standards that would make the traditional product obsolete.[45] The same light bulb that

> "If the American people needed another example of why it is time to roll back the hyper-regulation of the past four years, this is it. Washington banned a perfectly good product and fired hard working Americans based on little more than their own whim and the silly notion that they know better than the American consumer. Now, hundreds more Americans are looking for work while assembly lines in China are churning out fluorescent bulbs for the US market. Tell me how that makes any sense at all." –Marsha Blackburn (TN-R), who is currently working to repeal the light bulb ban

Entrepreneurship

revolutionized American industrialism and epitomizes the genuine grandeur of individual entrepreneurship. Why?

According to the government, the new florescent light bulbs, though more expensive, are much more energy efficient and save consumers more money on their energy bills. In other words: the government knows what's best for you and is graciously using the force of law to limit your own freedom and individual choices. How thoughtful of them! But why, you might ask, is this so controversial if it saves consumers money? The answer is threefold: First is the preposterous idea that the federal government has any authority to outlaw a specific item that has no effect on public safety. Does the government's opinion that something is beneficial for us justify a broach against our liberty to *choose*? Outlawing drugs is one thing (an obvious threat to public safety), but light bulbs? That brings me to the second point: there are legitimate safety concerns against the new florescent light bulbs. Containing mercury, the new 'energy efficient' bulbs are highly dangerous and not so efficient when it comes to human health.[46a] There is also a tedious process involved when one of these bulbs breaks.[47b] So not only does this government

---

[a] According to The Scientific American, "a single broken bulb in a Maine household trigger the state's Department of Environmental Protection to refer the homeowner to a decontaminator." Also, "a 1987 article in *Pediatrics* describes a 23-month-old who suffered weight loss and severe rashes after a carton of eight-foot (2.4-meter) tubular bulbs broke in a play area."

[b] After a mercury light bulb breaks, the EPA recommends first opening all the windows and doors and removing all people and pets from the room for 15 minutes. Then, pick up big pieces with cardboard or gloves (on a carpet

First Principles for my First Election

intervention act in a manner not involving public safety, it introduces an issue of public safety where there was none! The third point is both practically based and highly symbolic. The new florescent bulbs are nearly all made in China (posing another possible security risk). More importantly however, this transition would inevitably lead to the loss of American jobs –including the very last light bulb factory in the country. How symbolic this is! The light bulb –the very embodiment of American ingenuity and creativity- lost to an unnecessary government regulation that limits consumer choice, hurts American jobs, and introduces real health concerns all in the name of energy efficiency. Could this symbolize the government "turning out the lights" on American ingenuity?

Throughout our history Americans have had the 'I'll-do-it-myself' attitude of a staunch individualist. As previously stated, it was this spirit that led to the young Republic to enormous growth and eventually the world's greatest superpower. When Alexis de Tocqueville, a Frenchmen, came to tour the American continent in the early 1800's, he left with such a deep impression of appreciation of the American people that he wrote a book on its unique culture and lifestyle that differed so much from the dull and uninteresting life of the Europeans.[c] Among topics he

---

surface). Use duct tape to pick up the smaller pieces. Place the contents in a glass jar with a metal lid so that the fumes do not spread. Then, dispose of the contents at a special recycling plant (since throwing it in the garbage is illegal in most areas). These recycling plants are usually miles away.
[c] For a full analysis on Tocqueville's experience in America, read his book

Entrepreneurship

addressed was his astonishment at "the spirit of enterprise" that so characterized the people he encountered. He writes, "Almost all of them are real industrial entrepreneurs."[48] History proves the truth of Tocqueville's kind words. That fervent spirit of independence is seen in the Revolution when the colonists dared to defend their liberty against the largest military power of the colonial era. It is seen in the adventurous and bold pioneers that trekked westward in search of land and opportunity. It is seen in the Industrial Revolution in the early 20th century.

Now we are at the dawn of a new age and from all fair accounts, it looks as if that potential for entrepreneurial achievement is being smothered by government intervention. The light bulb is only the tip of the iceberg. Government is stunting growth in every sector of the economy, and at the same time making us more dependent on Chinese goods. [49d] Americans used to MAKE things! We invented the light bulb, the refrigerator, the airplane, the computer, and the radio –all signature symbols of our entrepreneurial spirit. We were a nation of thinkers, of inventors, of entrepreneurs! We used to be self-reliant as a nation.

Democracy in America.
[d] Dependence on Chinese goods is especially concerning. Not only are their human rights concerns with purchasing goods made from forced child labor under unthinkable working conditions, but there are also safety risks as numerous recalled toys have tested positively with lead poisoning. Others say that dependency on China economically could have serious national security implications, implying that the U.S. government could be influenced in the decision making process if Chinese interests ever conflict with that of our own.

First Principles for my First Election

So what happened? One answer could be that American's have simply lost their drive for innovation and for the advancement of the human condition. Perhaps we are just too lazy. Perhaps we are perfectly content where we are and have lost the spirit of independence once and for all. This is one idea, but the facts are not generally supportive of it. Studies show that an overwhelming majority of 60-70% of Americans wish they could work for themselves –to be their own boss. 84% of Americans say they'd be more passionate about their work if they ran their own business.[50] Clearly it's not a lack of enthusiasm that is preventing people from being entrepreneurs. So what is?

All signs point to the government. Government

> "The goal of price controls like the minimum wage is essentially to repeal the law of supply and demand, but senators might as well try to repeal the law of gravity. Worse than folly, disrupting the equilibrium of Labor markets causes economic damage. Although the minimum wage will not work according to economic theory-and it has not worked in reality-what makes it especially tragic is that it hits poor Americans hardest."
>
> Kane, T. (2005, March 4). *Minimizing economic opportunity by raising the minimum wage.* Retrieved from http://www.heritage.org/research/reports/2005/03/minimizing-economic-opportunity-by-raising-the-minimum-wage?query=Minimizing Economic Opportunity by Raising the Minimum Wage

intervention does not stop at the light bulb. The tentacles of the Leviathan invasively reach into nearly every corner of society

Entrepreneurship

including business, energy, and education, and the labor market.[e] Take for example, minimum wage laws.

Another progressive invention, minimum wage laws have a proven track record of complete failure. Contrived to make the evil business owners pay their workers decent wages, the laws were enacted over a century ago. Unfortunately, they are still in effect, despite the fact that the business culture has adapted and wages continue to rise. The minimum wage protections of the government are now outdated and effectively useless. In fact, minimum wage laws actually have a *negative* impact –hurting the most disadvantaged among us: the poor, unskilled laborers, and *the youth*!

Simple economics shows us that if businesses, especially small businesses, are required by law to pay employees an amount artificially higher than the equilibrium price of a wage, those businesses will have to compensate in other areas. Each time the government increases minimum wage, employers are forced to layoff employees or bring in fewer new hires. A minimum wage acts as a price floor, and when applied to the laws of supply and demand, it causes a decrease in the quantity of labor demanded. This hurts the businesses and the workers. Businesses lose money and would-be workers remain on the unemployment list. The first to go when it comes to layoffs or rejecting new hires is the youth.

---

[e] Leviathan is a literary term used by political scientists to describe a government –usually in a negative way, referring to its monstrous qualities, such as its ability to expand in power and take liberty from its citizens.

First Principles for my First Election

We are expendable in the eyes of most employers when the budget gets tight and companies are forced to tighten their belts. Also, the youth are most adversely affected by this since an overwhelming majority of the youth work for small businesses. An academic publication called the *Journal of Economic Perspectives,* reported that 71% of surveyed economists affirmed that "a minimum wage increases unemployment among the young and unskilled."[51] Even more telling however, are the statistics released by the Employment Policies Institute that reveal a 2.7-4.3% increase in teen unemployment for every 10% increase in the minimum wage. Among those working for small businesses, the number of unemployed teens doubles to 4.6-9.0%.

Yet, conventional wisdom disregards these facts –instead holding on to more simplistic and fanciful notions. *Government is nice. Government helps people. Therefore, government imposed minimum wage laws help people.* So, for my fellow Millennials who may still be skeptical or confused about the above evidence that minimum wage laws *hurt* the youth and unskilled workers, consider its history: Minimum wage laws were *created* to hurt the poor and blacks. They were *created* to protect skilled, white labor. Yes, that's right; the idea of implementing minimum wage laws in America was conceived as a racist plot to protect white union workers from having to compete with lower-skilled blacks. The Davis-Bacon Act of 1931 created a minimum wage[f] for any

---

[f] Then called a "prevailing wage"

Entrepreneurship

construction projects that received funds from the federal government. Because the wage was set at the price of unionized labor, non-union workers –consisting mostly of blacks at the time- were either laid off by contractors or not hired at all to save the cost of labor. Therefore, the very purpose of this minimum wage law when it was enacted was to deny blacks and lower skilled workers jobs, so how can anyone argue that these types of laws don't do this today?[52] [53]

In fact, this could be part of the reason that the black unemployment rate, as of this writing, is near 16% (double that of the white unemployment rate), and the reason that the unemployment rate for black Millennials hit 46.5% last August –a 25 year record high.[54] How can President Obama and his Democratic Party claim to be the defenders of blacks and the poor and still advocate for economic policies such as the minimum wage that cripple this segment of the population, smothering economic growth and stunting entrepreneurial spirit?[g]

Regulations on business, such as the minimum wage, impose barriers to economic success and large deterrents for would-be entrepreneurs. Instead of Millennials and other aspiring

---

[g] This very tactic has been used not only in the United States, but also in South Africa and Canada (to disadvantage Japanese citizens). Some have suggested that the reason Democratic Congressman, even black members of congress, continue to support minimum wage laws is because unions such as the AFL-CIO and SEIU are among the biggest financial donors to the Democratic Party. For more information about how the minimum wage has been used as an instrument of racism, read Thomas Sowell's book *South Africa's War Against Capitalism*.

First Principles for my First Election

Americans pursuing their dreams and launching their own career path, they cower in the face of government red tape. Few have the financial means to pay such expenses involved in starting a new company these days. This inhibits innovation and bright young minds from making a difference in their community.

    Another failure of the United States government on behalf of Millennials is the decline of academic opportunity in the fields of science, technology, engineering, and math (STEM programs) throughout the public education system. As explained in a previous chapter, all levels of the American public education system (elementary, secondary, and post-secondary) have strayed from their first principles. Whereas education in America used to encourage enlightenment, empowerment, and entrepreneurship, it has deteriorated into a chaotic bureaucracy managed by powerful teachers' unions and political elites. It is well documented that the STEM disciplines have been devastated by this apparent lack of focus, and because of this many generations of young people have been deprived the academic opportunity to pursue careers in these fields.

    Positions of science, technology, engineering, and math are essential to the vitality of the American Republic. It was the drive of entrepreneurial spirit and the favorable business climate of our country that elevated us as the leaders of the free world. The Industrial Revolution of the 1800's saw a boom in the progress of science and technology as America's creative genius

Entrepreneurship

(personified by Thomas Edison) was unleashed. Science and technology grew this country, and they are equally important today.

Conservatives are often condemned as "anti-science." In fact, while we were discussing the 2012 election between classes, a teacher told me that he would not support a social conservative (referring to candidate Michele Bachmann) in the general election because, according to him, social conservatives are "anti-science." There could be nothing further from the truth. The fact that conservatives believe in eternal, foundational principles, doesn't mean that we oppose the progress and the advancement of science. As Russell Kirk put it, "Permanence and progression are not enemies, for there can be no improvement except upon a sound foundation, and that foundation cannot endure unless it is progressively renewed."[55] So we see that principles and progress are complements and are essential to the preservation of ordered liberty.

Now that we live in a globalist economy it is perhaps even more important that our society maintains a vibrant enthusiasm for math and science programs. Having a large class of entrepreneurs leading the world in technological advances will give us a competitive advantage in global markets and will create thousands of new jobs here at home.

Likewise, technology is becoming increasingly important on the national security front. The U.S. government needs bright

First Principles for my First Election

young minds that will be able to offset the threat of a nuclear attack by utilizing our sophisticated missile defense technologies. Also, as cyber security becomes more necessary, the United States will require the creative brains and entrepreneurial spirit of the greatest minds in the world to stay one step ahead of our nation's cyber enemies.[56h]

Unfortunately, due to decades of cultural and political neglect of STEM initiatives, America no longer leads the world in math and science. According to the Organization for Economic Cooperation and Development (OECD), the U.S. ranked a mere average ranking among the 65 major countries evaluated. Among the top scorers in math and science were Shanghai and Hong Kong, China, South Korea, Singapore, Finland and Japan. The U.S. followed significantly –receiving an average score in math and below average in science.[57] This is also reflected in the decreasing number of students pursuing a STEM degree in college, which has dropped from 32% in 1995 to 27% in 2004.

---

[h] "In 2006, Chinese intelligence agencies covertly attacked at least four separate U.S. government computer networks. In June 2007, 150 computers in the $1.75 billion computer network at the U.S. Department of Homeland Security were quietly penetrated by programs that sent an unknown quantity of information to a Chinese-language Web site. In the same month of June 2007, Chinese military hackers circumvented one of the Defense Department's computer networks. The skills necessary for China to engage in this type of cyber warfare are a direct result of the ingenuity of STEM-educated Chinese citizens. The new technologies and techniques America needs to combat these types of attacks depend on America's ability to produce citizens with superior STEM skills."

Entrepreneurship

Moreover, one third of those earning a STEM degree were of foreign students studying abroad.[58]

There are cultural as well as political reasons for America's decline in the mathematical and scientific entrepreneurship. I have witnessed the cultural disconnect in my own high school. All of my upper level math and science classes are dominated by foreign students. My high school is predominantly white, but we have representation from a wide variety of ethnic groups and most of these students of foreign descent comprise most of the higher level academic classes. For instance, my AP[i] Chemistry class was divided exactly between whites and non-whites. In that class I new people of Indian, Korean, Chinese, Nigerian, and Argentinean descent. Similarly, this trend held true for my AP Calculus BC class, which consisted of many Asian students. This reflects a cultural disconnect between Americans and the STEM disciplines. For some reason, respect and appreciation of the math and sciences has been diminishing in America, even while increasing around the world. Of course, there are still many American-born citizens who still dream of becoming a rocket-scientist or a brain-surgeon, but the facts show that they are dwindling in numbers. Perhaps this is due to the ever increasing entitlement mentality of modern society.

---

[i] AP stands for Advanced Placement –students take an AP exam administered by the College Board to receive college credit for the class

First Principles for my First Election

Another reason for the decline of the STEM initiatives, and a more likely one at that, is the federal government's attack on scientific entrepreneurship. Not only have STEM programs been reduced and diminished on the local level by our incompetent public school systems, but they have also been under assault on the national level, even by the President himself. In his 2011 budget, President Obama eliminated Constellation -a major portion of NASA's space program- ditching the nearly $10 billion investment as a sunk cost. [59] At a time when we should be encouraging young people to pursue STEM professions, the government is visibly attacking these industries either through excessive regulation or budget cuts. This, combined with public schools' systematic devaluation of the STEM disciplines, has dramatically hurt scientific entrepreneurship for future generations.

The solution to restoring scientific entrepreneurship is not more federal spending, however. The best that could be done is to provide more opportunity for students in elementary and high school to pursue their interests in math and science. The education bureaucracy needs to be reformed (if not eliminated altogether) so that state and local school systems can refocus on these key areas in math and science, and thus provide students with more academic opportunity. Government should step out of the way and let the creative genius of the American spirit run wild.

Entrepreneurship

Now that we have witnessed a couple of battles in government's war on entrepreneurship, let's examine another regulation that affects every individual in America. The overwhelming percentage of government regulations come from *one* regulation agency: The Environmental Protection Agency.[j] The history of the EPA is actually quite simple: After a decade of pot-smoking, free love, and hippie peace marches, the radical environmental movement was born on April 22nd, 1970 –and that's according to the EPA's own government website! Seriously.

"American environmentalism dawned as a popular movement on a mild spring afternoon in 1970. Wednesday, April 22nd, brought blue skies, light breezes, and temperatures in the 60s to New York City and Washington, D.C. Much of the rest of the country enjoyed similar conditions. On that day, the influence of nature had particular meaning; the nation held a celebration of clean air, land, and water. Encouraged by the retreat of winter, millions participated."[60]

The pot-smoking bit wasn't a joke either.

---

[j] $23 billion out of the $26.5 billion of the 43 new rules and regulations (just put into effect in 2010!

First Principles for my First Election

"...marijuana smoke may have hung in wisps over some of the day's festivities, but violence and confrontation were nowhere to be seen."[61]

So there you have it! The green movement was born from the dreams of...well...college hippies singing kumbaya who eventually grew up, bathed, lost the tie-dye and became college professors. After the launch of Earth Day, the green movement took off, leading a Republican, President Richard Nixon to create the Environmental Protection Agency in 1970 (later to be expanded by liberal President Jimmy Carter).

Do not misunderstand. There is nothing inherently wrong with Millennials wanting a cleaner earth. There *is* something wrong with the government taking advantage of us by executing that ideal through an expensive agency that is both unconstitutional and proven to do more harm than good. The EPA is a prime example of how emotionally-charged, feel-good issues have severe negative consequences in the real world. The following examples show how an ideologically driven set of policies hurt *real* people and *real* businesses.

The most recent regulations imposed by the EPA will affect all automakers in the U.S. and every individual who happens to be in need of a car. According to new efficiency standards, all automakers will be required by law to report a fleet-wide average fuel economy level of 54.5 mpg by model year 2025

Entrepreneurship

for passenger cars, light-duty trucks, and medium-duty passenger vehicles. The new regulation will dictate specific fuel efficiency standards by model type, weighted by sales volume. This will require significantly greater investment in re-engineering. In addition, there is a renewed crackdown on tailpipe carbon dioxide emissions (for the scientifically uninitiated, carbon dioxide is the gas you exhale when you breathe...suspect number one for the cause of global warming, or is it climate change now?). These new regulations are estimated to result in an increase from $2,000-$3,100 on the sticker price of every vehicle in the U.S![62] Automakers will be forced to find a financial means to meet these new standards in a relatively short period of time. The burden of costs will not rest on them however, but on us, the Millennials. Some analysts predict this will actually increase the amount of pollution! By increasing sticker prices, "Consumers are thus more likely to hold on to older, more polluting cars."[63] Whether better gas mileage will save drivers more money in the long run is debatable. Fuel efficiency relies on a host of variable factors such as model type, local weather conditions, and driving habits. One thing is for certain: these regulations will add to the cost of business, will restrict entrepreneurial success, and will leech the pocket books of the American people.

    Energy production is also hindered by unnecessary government intervention in the economy. Expanding off-shore drilling and nuclear energy in order to become energy independent

First Principles for my First Election

and to lower gas prices are popular ideas with the American people,[64k] but they are blocked by extensive regulations. Despite the erroneous description of the 'dangers' involved with energy production preached by radical disciples of the green movement, one fact remains: Americans need oil, and Americans will get oil. The only factor that is up for debate is whether we should produce our own oil or buy it at extremely high prices set by OPEC –a group of oil-rich countries in the Middle East that hate our guts. Drilling for American oil would relieve us of a major national security threat (that being reliant on our enemies for energy), would simultaneously put tens of thousands of Americans companies to work –entrepreneurship, and would instantly lower gas prices as the supply of oil increased. It's simple economics.

> "Listening to liberals invoke the sanctity of "science" to promote their crackpot ideas creates the same uneasy feeling as listening to Bill Clinton cite Scripture. Who are they kidding? Liberals hate science. Science might produce facts impervious to their crying and hysterics. Even at college re-education camps, it's striking that the chemical engineering and economics departments are jam-packed with Republicans, while liberals are all taking French." –Godless by Ann Coulter, page 172

Likewise, many Americans are supportive of nuclear energy.[l] It is highly efficient and 100% eco-friendly as it produces *no* carbon emissions. The technology is proven to be safe and the

---

[k] Gallup polling shows that 60% of Americans support offshore drilling.
[l] An overwhelming 58% of Americans agree that nuclear energy is safe.

Entrepreneurship

only incidents that have induced thoughts otherwise were caused by human error.[65] Another benefit is that the waste produced by nuclear reactors is extremely small and can be easily stored until it naturally decays. Some of the waste can even be recycled and used for the production of energy. Moreover, France (yes that France) has 58 reactors that produce 80% of the entire nation's energy! Since when have we ever let *France* beat us at anything? Because of regulations that make it virtually impossible to build a new nuclear power plant, the U.S., only runs on 15% nuclear energy.[66] If not for these regulations, thousands of jobs could be created for the operation of new power plants. These facts show another example of how government –particularly the EPA- can stifle job growth and hurt the economy. Moreover, it proves that government is the biggest obstacle to the thriving spirit of Millennial ingenuity and scientific discovery.[m]

Another barrier to the emergence of entrepreneurs in the 21st century is the progressive tax code. It might come as a surprise to those who were educated in liberal indoctrination camps (otherwise known as public schools), such as myself, that our country did not legally have a national income tax for the first century of its existence. The U.S. government first began dabbling with the idea of a national income tax in 1861 during the Civil

---

[m] On that note, have you noticed the recurring theme that liberals are absolutely married to their god Science until it presents an opportunity to advance scientific technology and with it, the human condition?

First Principles for my First Election

War and thereafter to help pay for the Union's accumulated war debts. Though a direct tax by the national government was not technically legal,[n] politicians experimented with a tax rate ranging from 3-5% anyway on the wealthiest Americans (A rate which would be considered a joke today!) However, in 1895 the Supreme Court ruled 5-4 that the national income tax was ruled unconstitutional. It wasn't until 1913 that Congress and the States, guided by the progressive giants of Wilson, Roosevelt, and Taft, ratified a constitutional amendment that granted the federal government the authority to tax individual income.[67]

So how did our country become the world's greatest superpower by the turn of the century *without* an income tax? As we will see, the absence of a national income tax was actually one of the main reasons for the unprecedented growth of our capitalist economy. Meanwhile, the federal government operated on corporate taxes, tariffs on trade, excise taxes on alcohol, tobacco, firearms, taxes on military hardware sales, etc. There was simply no need to dip into people's pockets and deprive them of their earned wages. *But that was back then!* We are told. *Society has changed and now government is much more active in helping people, such as in areas of education and social welfare.*

It might still surprise those who continue to regurgitate this argument that there are many states even today that operate without a state income tax. Yes in the 21st century! In fact there

---

[n] Due to Article 1 Section 9 of the Constitution

Entrepreneurship

are 9 states with no income tax, and my home state of Tennessee, I can proudly say, is one of them.º Popular opinion might hold that these backwards, foot dragging, Neolithic policies would be a drain on the respective states considering how much has changed in this country since the 1800's. Many hold the opinion that some states, especially in the South, are seriously behind when it comes to making financial ends meet. (On a personal note: one girl at my high school, who moved from California, was completely surprised when she arrived at a public school in Tennessee. She told her friends that she was absolutely convinced that none of them would be wearing shoes!) This stereotype couldn't be farther from the truth.

Tennessee was listed as number one in the country for being the most business-friendly state.[68p] And we still have shoes. We still have public schools, and we still have public roads and highways. We still offer welfare services. So how does it work? States without an income tax rely heavily on a state sales tax. While the other 41 states have both an income tax and a sales tax, the remaining nine are left with only the latter. Therefore, the amount of revenue the government brings in is directly proportional to the amount of consumer spending. This practically *forces* the state to be open and friendly to business so as to attract

---

º Alaska, Florida, Nevada, New Hampshire, South Dakota, Tennessee, Texas, Washington, and Wyoming have NO state income tax.
p Six of the nine states that have no state income tax were ranked in the "Top Ten States Most Friendly to Business" by the U.S. Chamber of Congress in 2011.

new jobs and spending within its borders. States like Tennessee do this by offering job-creating out-of-state companies to transfer to their state in exchange for temporary or long-lasting tax credits. The government sees the opportunity for job creation (thus widening the tax base) and spending as a greater benefit than taxing the perspective company. These states also rely on property taxes and other local taxes to supply the needed revenue. Again, most states have these taxes in addition to a state income tax, which places a heavier burden on the population, discouraging spending weakening the tax base. States with no income tax continue to outperform in every area of life. Texas for instance, is home to numerous business friendly policies enacted by a conservative legislature and Governor Rick Perry, whose state excelled as the nation's largest exporting state and in 2011 it led the nation in job creation.[69]

Unfortunately, most states are not sheltered by these policies of economic conservatism. Even the states who are most friendly to business cannot escape the reach of the federal government which simply does not reflect the values of entrepreneurship and fiscal responsibility. Rather than learning from the successes and failures of the 50 states –the supposed "laboratories of democracy"- the feds firmly entrench themselves in rigid ideologically driven economic and tax policies that stunt growth and douse the burning desire for entrepreneurship. The federal government *does* have a national income tax that reaches

Entrepreneurship

everyone regardless of the location on the map.[70][q] In addition, the United States has the 2nd highest corporate tax rat in the world at an astounding 35%.[71] Is this Washington's way of attracting businesses to the U.S.?

The policies in Washington have resulted in a decrease in the economic freedom of our country, which will have disastrous effects on Millennials in the future. The Heritage Foundation's 2011 Index of Economic Freedom downgraded the U.S. to the 9th freest economy which lowers our standing from "free" to "mostly free." According to their calculations based on a country's business freedom, trade freedom, fiscal freedom, government spending, etc. The U.S. is gradually slipping from its place at the top of the economic ladder. High taxes on both individuals and corporations and high unemployment, coupled with high government spending and regulatory scheming, have resulted in this downgrade in our economic freedom.

Most reasonable people at this point are probably wondering one simple question: Why? Why does the government continue policies if they aren't working? Why does the government hinder growth and entrepreneurs from emerging to save our economy? Why aren't states recognized for their effective polices? The answer is found in the words of our own President.

---

[q] Unless you are a multi-billion dollar corporation that just happens to donate millions to Washington insiders, like GE or Goldman Sachs who donated $528,180 and $1,012,841 alone to the Obama campaign in 2008.

First Principles for my First Election

We are constantly lectured by our public officials that "the rich need to pay their fair share" and that a good government should "spread the wealth around" as then-candidate Barack Obama said on the campaign trail in 2008. When confronted by Joe Wurzelbacher, a local plumber, about the harmful effects of Obama's proposed tax policy on his business, Obama responded, "It's not that I want to punish your success; I just want to make sure that everybody who is behind you that they've got a chance to success, too. I think when you spread the wealth around, it's good for everybody."[72]

This gives deep insight into the true motives behind the economic policies of the elites in Washington. When asked about his tax policy, Obama did not respond by saying that he was focused on and creating a business climate favorable to young entrepreneurs; he responded with an adamant belief in a redistributive ideology. He, like other politicians, is more concerned with redistributing income –taking from the "rich" and giving to the poor. The past Obama administration's class warfare tactics over the past three years have been a testament to that fact.

I believe that if Millennials can see through the historical lies about the nature of business, if we begin to denounce the transition of our country from a vibrant Republic to a Regulatory State. If we can ignore the redistributive politics of class warfare, we will be able to not only rescue this nation from its economic

Entrepreneurship

misery, but we will also be able to spearhead a new era of growth, innovation, and genuine prosperity. Despite the hurdles and hoops the government has put in our way, they are no match for the raging enthusiasm of the younger generation. The Millennial generation is a generation of ideas. We have talent, creativity, and drive for success. It is the American way, and we are certainly no less American than our elders.

Of course Washington will have to get its act together and reform existing barriers to economic success and innovation in the market place. Economic policy will have to change and transition from an antiquated and burdensome view of business into a dynamic force for good that will strip away the regulations and taxation that impedes our generation from spurring real growth;[73r] but principles must come first.

On our side of the bargain, Millennials must continue our sustained energy for entrepreneurial innovation and drive for success. I have no doubt that the rising generation is capable of unleashing an incomparable amount creative potential, whether in areas of art, music, culture, technology, innovation, or business. All of us have different natural abilities, interests, and talents. Whether you are the next Edison or Mozart, the next Socrates or the next Bill Gates, whether you are an inventor or a musician, a

---

[r] According to the Heritage Foundation, the best action Congress could take to protect Americans from overregulation would be to "require congressional approval of new major rules promulgated by agencies, create a Congressional Office of Regulatory Analysis to review proposed and existing rules independently, and establish a sunset date for federal regulations."

First Principles for my First Election

philosopher or a businessman, we can *all* be entrepreneurs. We can all pursue our dreams and pursue our ambitions. We can all work to be the best in our field and to excel at what we love.

Whether you start your own restaurant or launch your own law firm, whether you invent the next "i-gadget" or explore outer space, whether you write your own book or own your own construction company, all of us are capable of greatness. As long as the government steps out of the way and we the people are free to pursue our own interests, the entrepreneurial spirit of the Millennials will be more than enough to lift this nation out of despair. Luckily, it looks like we are not in short supply. Studies show that "nearly 80% of would-be entrepreneurs in the United States are between the ages of 18 and 34!" This spirit of entrepreneurship is consistent among teenagers, 69% of whom want to become entrepreneurs even knowing the difficult path to self-employment and business creation.[74]

So the gap in the lack of job creation and slacking innovations of the 21st century is clearly not due to a lack of motivation on the part of the American people, it is the inevitable consequence of an intrusive government that squelches economic freedom and principled entrepreneurship so enshrined by the Millennial generation. Artificially built up by fanciful stories of evil corporations and contrived strife between rich and poor, the government has sold us a string of policies that outright don't work. There's simply no other way to put it. Over-regulation and

Entrepreneurship

excessive taxation always fail to accomplish what their makers intended to accomplish –unless of course their makers actually want to douse the flame of entrepreneurial spirit which is burning to create, invent, and explore.

Millennials are no less ingenious, no less creative, and no less passionate than those who came before us. I have no doubt that I live and work with people who have the potential to change the world. One of my friends, Zach Freeman, decided that he needed to do something to speak out against liberal indoctrination on college campuses. He felt the need to give young conservatives a voice in the fight for liberty, since we are so often drowned out by liberal teachers, professors, and other students on campus. In a bold effort of entrepreneurial spirit he started his own blog – TheCollegeConservative.com. I was honored to be one of the first people he asked to write for him. I wasn't quite sure what I was getting into when I signed up for the job, but I had the curiosity to find out; I also had faith that Zach would carry this project to great ends.

Just a few months later, what had started as a cheap internet blog created by a handful of college students, had turned into a sophisticated, thriving outlet for young conservatives from around the country to share thoughts and explore new ideas, safe from the clutches of liberal educators. The site now boasts of nearly 50 members on its writing staff (representing college students from coast to coast) and reports over 1 million all time

First Principles for my First Election

page views! Editors have secured interviews with radio hosts, newspapers, and major television programs such as The Today Show. This enterprise requires a lot of work on behalf of the writers who are expected to maintain high quality articles, but it is especially time consuming for the editing staff led by Zach and a few other co-editors. Needless to say, one person's entrepreneurial spirit successfully launched a technological revolution against the established liberal order of academia and gave conservatives from across the nation a platform to be heard. That is entrepreneurship at its finest.

    Zach will no doubt achieve great success someday, but he is not an anomaly. Americans all over the country share his passion and energy to create, to invent, and to lead; the difference between him and them, is simply the fact that he did it. Would-be-entrepreneurs are not rare; I can think of many that I know personally right off the top of my head. Several of my friends have the intelligence, drive, and potential to be the next Einstein. Others I know are fantastic writers and have it within themselves to enrich the literary world with untold talent. Still others I've met might as well be dressed in a suit and tie because of their assured position in the business community in the future. And I'm sure every reader of this book can identify with someone they know in their own life, if not with themselves, who has the potential for such greatness. It is within all of us, this spirit of entrepreneurship. It is the principle that an individual, undeterred by the forces of

Entrepreneurship

tyranny, can unleash his creative potential to advance the condition of himself and his fellow man leaving the world better than he found it. What better place to discover this concept and wield its power! The United States remains, at least for now, the land of opportunity. Millennials need to follow the lead set by those like Zach Freeman, who capitalized on the opportunity offered to them and translated that *spirit* of entrepreneurship into *action*. I encourage all Millennials to find within themselves that spirit and let Providence breathe fresh air into your sails that you might travel high and far.

Principle #4

Self-Reliance

John Stossel condemns America as "a nation of freeloaders" –and with good reason.[75] Ever since the booming prosperity and economic opportunity of the post WWII era, Americans have spoiled themselves and their children. We have not only become obsessed with material possessions and services, but now demand that we have a *right* to them –that we are *entitled*. This mentality has led to an explosion of government power as a means to provide for these entitlements –the things which most Americans now view as birthrights such as; financial assistance, education, healthcare, retirement funds, etc. There is a growing belief that government exists to take care of us, to baby us, to help us from cradle to grave. And thus the Nanny State was born.

First Principles for my First Election

The current nanny state style of government we have today was the brainchild of early 19th century progressive intellectuals, like Woodrow Wilson, who greatly admired the European style of socialism across the Atlantic. To them, government was a great good –the greatest good- that could advance the condition of man and to initiate 'progress.' It is very important to understand that these early 19th century intellectuals believed that man was inherently stupid, foolish, and incapable of living his life to his full potential if left to his own devices. They believed that man could not rule himself. Thus, a superior, enlightened government must take the yoke of responsibility from the poor, helpless, masses and "nudge" them in the right direction.[76a] It must provide for man's education, his wealth, his health, etc. All the while, the government, with its superior class of educated individuals, could redistribute the wealth of people more equally, more fairly. However, in order for the government to carry out these utopian socialist schemes, it needed growing room. So as the century progressed the government gradually, under both Democrats and Republicans, became larger and larger, expanding to fill the roles of life which man could simply not perform himself. Especially seizing power during times of

---

[a] Frighteningly enough, Cass Sustein, President Obama's regulatory czar wrote a book called *Nudge*, expressing these exact sentiments, detailing the best ways of manipulating the ignorant masses and molding them closer into the government's desire.

Self Reliance

national crises, such as the Great Depression or the two World Wars, the government became bigger and bigger while man's liberty became smaller and smaller.

It was not until the 1960's that this movement truly picked speed and began to push for radical political, moral, and cultural change. It was then that the feeling of entitlement took root in the nation's soul. The government launched itself into the business of social engineering –the process of intentionally reconstructing society based upon some preconceived, utopian ideal. President Johnson initiated the so-called "War on Poverty" –a noble but laughingly impractical plan to eliminate

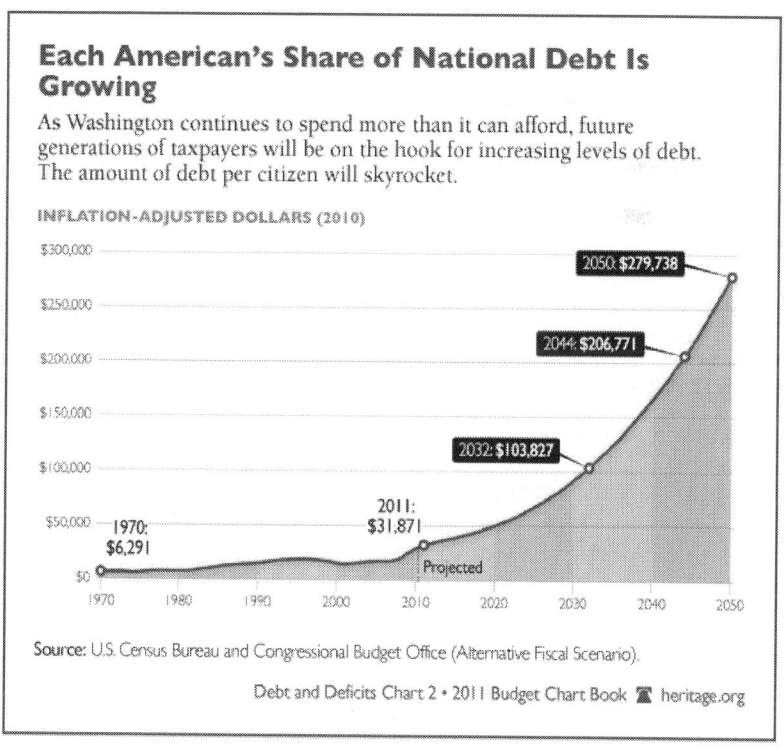

First Principles for my First Election

poverty. An explosion of entitlements and spending, which aimed at helping the poor, elderly, and unfortunate, instead created *more* poor people and buried the nation under a mountain of debt. Under President Carter the feds began to meddle in education, which after 40 years of hindsight have proven ineffective resulting in flat line test scores.

Even despite this failed history, moves have been made to improve education through federal intervention by President Bush in his unpopular No Child Left Behind Act. President Obama, on the other hand, has done considerably worse damage to the country by quadrupling spending, and introducing an entire new entitlement, known notoriously as Obamacare. [77]

And so, the joyride that previous generations have taken on the train to socialism has come to a stop and we are left with the bill: a 15 TRILLION dollar debt (that's **$15,000,000,000,000**) and growing, fast. In fact, in 2011 when the numbers are broken down, each man, woman, and child in America owed $31,871 on the national debt. At the rate of spending, that amount is set to triple in just 20 years. Below is a chart detailing the amount owed by every individual and its exponential growth unless reforms are put into place. [78]

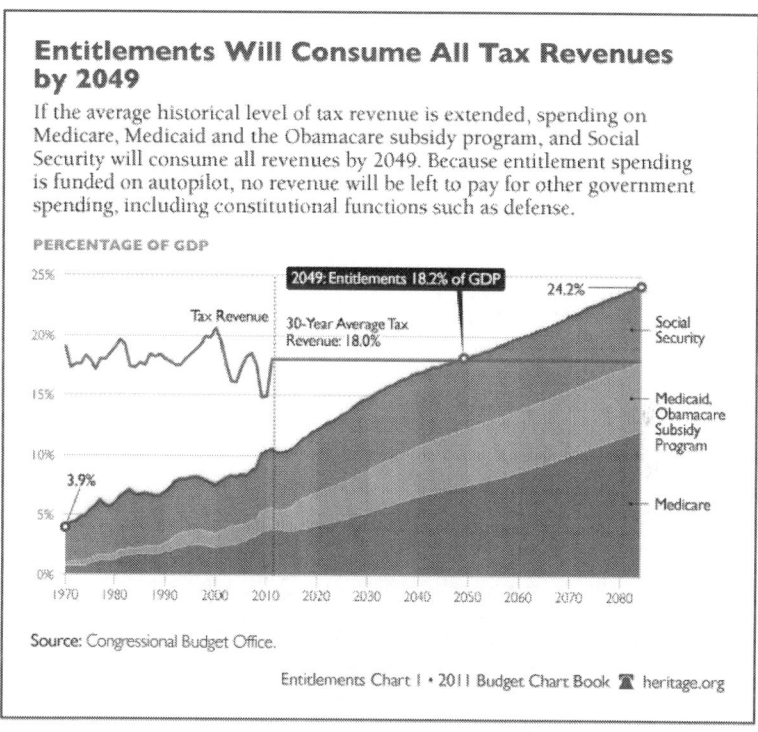

And despite their luxurious appeal (free education, free healthcare, welfare for the needy, and financial aid for the elderly), entitlements are the biggest contributor to the national debt, our national debt. This next chart shows that if entitlement spending continues to increase at the current rate, they *alone* will consume all tax revenue by 2049, leaving literally NO room for government to fulfill its rightful and constitutional obligations like providing for the common defense.

First Principles for my First Election

Still, our generation is left with the remains of an entitlement minded mentality that screams "Me, me, me! Mine, mine, mine!" despite the pending economic disaster. You don't have to be an economist to understand that our debt and entitlement spending is unsustainable.

So the question is this: Do we, as Millennials, continue this train ride to socialism, grabbing all the benefits we can get along the way, hoping for the best as we chug toward the cliff of inevitable consequences, or do we change this culture of entitlement, both in public policy and in our hearts? I choose the latter.

Evil cannot be defeated by ambivalence. To defeat evil requires good. In the same way, the entitlement mindset of our generation and of those before us must be replaced by some other motivation. Something good –self-reliance.

Big-government progressives detest self-reliance. Instead, they cherish every opportunity to make the population dependent upon them. They are the masters; we are the slaves. Of course, they don't say it quite like that. Government bureaucrats are brilliant at dressing up their schemes of dependency as being to your advantage. They tell you that you could not survive without them. They are wiser; they are more intelligent; they have the means; only through the collective can success be achieved, they say. Dependency.

Self Reliance

FDR knew a little something about dependency. As mentioned earlier, progressives have longed used the tactic of expanding government power and influence during times of crises. FDR, though not the father of this strategy, used it skillfully. At a time when millions were out of work, hungry, and in an overall desperate state, the government stepped in as the savior. Promising immediate relief and long term recovery, FDR launched a series of unprecedented power-grabs, both into the economy and government itself. Though his New Deal programs failed to reverse the Depression (and in some cases made it worse), they succeeded in establishing a new era of big government. Destroying the free market, Roosevelt attempted to create a new one based on progressive values such as those articulated in his proposed 'second bill of rights.' This revolutionary proposal, which never actually came to fruition, demanded for every American a job, a house, decent wage, among other inventions which he claimed were inalienable *rights*. Sound familiar?

FDR knew the powerful lure of security and the return for order. All he had to do was dangle the carrot of dependency and he miraculously had the entire nation running toward him. With this device he successfully won four elections (destroying the two-term tradition set by Washington), though he didn't live to finish the last. He was the closest thing we as Americans ever had to a king. And though he never turned the

First Principles for my First Election

economy around with his socialist policies (that would have to wait until the explosion of industry that came with WWII), he was remarkably popular. Why? He had mastered the art of dependency. He had the entire nation at his feet pleading for relief. And yet even Roosevelt understood the inherent evil of dependency: In 1935, he said:

"Continued dependence upon relief induces a spiritual and moral disintegration fundamentally destructive to the national fibre. To dole out relief in this way is to administer a narcotic, a subtle destroyer of the human spirit."[79]

    A culture of *dependence* is both uneconomical (as proven by the failed attempts of FDR's administration and virtually every subsequent government attempt to enslave the population through entitlements such as Johnson's Great Society and others), and immoral. To be dependent on another is to be a slave. Any teenager with a car can attest to that. Unless you can fully afford to buy your car, pay for your gas, and make payments on your insurance, most likely your parents have some sort of control over you and 'your' vehicle. They limit where you can go, with whom, and when. Why? Because they bought it! Same goes for college students. Parents have enormous weight and influence when they are helping pay tuition. That is dependency –enslavement. Even

Self Reliance

the Bible speaks to this concept in the book of Proverbs chapter 22: "The borrower is slave to the lender." It is true for the youth, and it is true for adults. Any form of dependency is a form of slavery. Or, as FDR blatantly states, dependency is a narcotic. Our nation has become addicted to entitlements. The Left in particular has become a violent defender of these so called 'rights.' Just as a drug user will do anything, and I mean anything to get his drugs, so too will the dependent defend entitlements. They will go through any means and pay any price (see our national debt) to get what they feel they are entitled to have. And just as overcoming an addiction takes serious time and powerful will, so too will it take our country to recover from this mindset that is literally bankrupting our nation's wallets and also our nation's soul.

When an individual comes to the point of self-sustainability and self-reliance and still borrows from or feeds off another, one could make a strong case that it is immoral. However, when one *demands* what is not theirs as an inherent *right*, it becomes without question an act of immoral behavior. In his book *Liberty and Learning*, Dr. Larry P. Arrn, the President of Hillsdale College illustrates the important distinction between 'rights' and privileges. Rights are common to all individuals as inalienable gifts which are endowed to us by our Creator. These rights include the right to life, liberty, and property. These are the most basic things we

First Principles for my First Election

own as humans. We have an inherent right to our lives and to defend them in self-defense. We have the right to liberty – to worship God how we see fit and to freely live as we please without bringing harm to others. Also we have the right to property –the fruits of our labor which are manifest by either physical things we create or by wages and the purchases we make with them.

These are things common to every individual and are universal truths that cannot be denied to anyone. Others, out of political motivation, invent new 'rights' that serve a certain agenda. These 'rights' can be quite deceptive and largely believable unless high scrutiny is given to them. Among these invented rights are the right to education and healthcare. These two things (among others) might be important, even a necessity, but they are not inherent rights. Not all things that are necessary are rights.

Mr. Arnn makes this distinction by comparing, or contrasting, the right to property with the 'right' to food (a necessity for every human being). Private property is a right because it is the direct result of your labor. If you build a house by your own hand, it is yours and no one else's. If you grow food in your garden, it belongs to only you. If you work for a business, you give them your time, energy, and ability, and thus you are rewarded with a wage for that invested work. That wage and whatever you choose to purchase with it is a

Self Reliance

direct fruit of your labor, and thus belongs to you and only you. Food, however necessary, cannot be put in this category. To say that you have a right to food implies that you are not responsible for growing, buying, or obtaining it. It is your *right*. You are *entitled* to it. Or as Mr. Arnn puts it...

"To assert that such rights exist [i.e. food] is to assert that another is required by his own efforts to provide them. But of course that sets up a conflict, even a war, between one citizen and another. It pits the right of each of us to the product of our own labor against that needs of our fellow citizens. To require another to labor for us that we may do well is, in fact, a form of slavery. As Abraham Lincoln said in his Second Inaugural Address: 'It is strange that some men should pray to a just God to wring their bread from the sweat of other men's faces.'"[80]

And thus the theory that the necessities of life are rights, such as food, education, and healthcare, is morally dismantled. In fact, to suggest that the government should intentionally shift the burden of cost and expense to the backs of others is in fact *im*moral. This is not to say that people, whether people of faith or not, do not have an individual and moral responsibility to help those who can't help themselves. We do! The act of charity is vital and necessary in a free and virtuous republic. That act however, was envisioned by our Founders to be from

First Principles for my First Election

the hands of private citizens and churches –not by the government. The government only exists to protect our natural rights. To go beyond that in word or deed is in fact slavery. And though the goals of entitlement programs are noble, the means are economically destructive and morally questionable. We cannot deceive ourselves by saying that there is such a thing as 'good slavery.' Many slaveholders justified their enslavement of blacks by suggesting that it was better for them. There was a longstanding prejudice that blacks were inherently inferior both intellectually and morally and would not be able to provide for themselves if set free. Blacks were of course not inferior beings and were equal under God just as any other man, but years of forced illiteracy and imposed ignorance by their owners did pose as a formidable obstacle to true freedom. Even after the Civil War blacks had a difficult time assimilating to freedom in America. So in a way, this was partially true. It was a noble, yet twisted thought. So did that make slavery any less wrong? No! Dependence, especially the involuntary kind, is always wrong. Morally it is wrong for the dependent, and economically it is wrong for the one left paying the bill.

Such is the nature of dependency: weakness, destruction, enslavement. This comes from the words of a President who so masterfully utilized its effects (FDR) and a President who fought a bitter war and literally laid down his life to destroy it.

Self Reliance

But self-reliance is the spirit of *independence*! Not *dependence*. And bred into the blood of the American culture is a deep rooted spirit of independence. Since the Revolution, when the American colonists valiantly threw off the yoke of British tyranny, Americans have long had a record of keeping to themselves, living a private life, and providing for themselves and their families.

Even before the Revolution, the colonists lived virtually free and independent for the most part of 200 years between the early settlement of Jamestown in 1607 and the birth of the new Republic in 1776. For nearly two centuries the Americans lived to themselves and enjoyed a long time of peace and self-governance under the crown's policy of salutary neglect, gradually building up a spirit of self-reliance and independence that, once challenged, would be vehemently defended.

The principle of self-reliance is not restrained in American history to our nation's early years however. We as Millennials can even see this principle by observing the lives of our grandparents and great-grandparents. It used to be commonly agreed upon that a responsible person should live within his means –not spending more than he earned and being frugal and thrifty with what he did earn. Now however it has become more popular to play the victim card in order to get artificial assistance.

First Principles for my First Election

In the adult world, "my dog ate my homework," excuses just don't cut it. But those perpetrators of irresponsible behavior, whom all of us encounter from grade school, still linger and ride on the backs of others, all the while, struggling to come up with more imaginative and elaborate excuses for their laziness. "My dog ate my homework" becomes "it's not my fault; I'm a victim of society!" As excuse after excuse is given, not only do the "victims" begin to believe their own lies, but as a result, the compassionate and caring heartstrings of many politicians are pulled until they cave –bowing to special interests while sacrificing the will of the majority.[b]

When it comes to devising a victim hood sob story, excuses can be very imaginative. Many tend to blame the circumstances into which they were born. If my parents are poor, then how can I ever live up to achieve my dreams? Some assert. They immediately throw out any possibility of earning a higher education, getting a well paying job, or becoming anything better than their parents, thus neglecting obvious opportunities offered by society such as academic and need-based scholarships, employment opportunities, or financial help from churches or other charitable organizations. They immediately turn to the government for a handout.

---

[b] For more in depth reading on the pandemic of Americans who cried, "victim!" read Ann Coulter's book *Guilty*.

Self Reliance

It is highly unfortunate for the children who are born into these circumstances, who suffer from bad choices not their own. In inner city public housing projects (or ghettoes) children often grow up without proper parenting (or perhaps more often without two parents at all). They do not have parents responsible enough to instill them with the desire to learn or to do well in school. Often, by their teenage years, the only escape from their lowly lifestyle that they can see is success in sports, drugs, or crime. Needless to say, it is not impossible to climb the socio-economic ladder of success from the bottom to the top. Rags to riches stories are not rare in America-the land of opportunity. It only requires self-discipline, motivation, and a fervent individualist spirit.

I take comfort in the stories from my own family's history. Neither my mom, nor my dad (now divorced and both remarried), could afford to go to college after graduating high school. My dad went straight to the police department at 21 years old (and still works as a police offer today, over 20 years later.). Later in her life, my mom went to school at night (while working full-time) to take technology classes. She earned an associate's degree and has worked over 20 years in IT for an insurance company.

Even my step-dad, and step-mom who both went to college, had to work for every cent. My step-dad joined the Marine Corps and returned four years later to get a college

First Principles for my First Election

education. With no help from his parents, he worked his way through 4 years of college at Murray State University. My step-mom also growing up in a low income family, managed to secure several federal grants based on her financial need and the fact that she had studied her way to 3rd in her high school class. She went on to Middle Tennessee State University, then to graduate school where she got a Master's degree. All of my parents were more fortunate than their parents and grandparents.

Nearly all of my great-grandparents lived on farms, where they were forced to become self-reliant. My grandmother's parents married as young teenagers and built their own house out in the country in Robertson County, TN. They grew their own food and made their own clothes. My grandmother and her sisters took baths in the creek. My dad's parents also grew up under similar circumstances, both of them in rural and poor conditions. Though neither could afford college, they both worked their way up the economic ladder and eventually started their own real estate business that prospered rapidly.

My family has set a high precedent for me, but nevertheless, they have proven that the American Dream is alive and well. I am blessed to live in Williamson County, TN and am blessed to have four encouraging voices that want to help elevate me to my highest potential.

Self Reliance

It is easy to play the victim card. It is easy to, when faced with extreme circumstances, to drop one's chin in defeat and walk away from one's dreams. This however, is pure cowardice and should not be encouraged, let alone by the government.

Concurrent with the principle of self-reliance, it is my position that the government should "help those who can't help themselves," but not those who refuse to help themselves. The disadvantaged should be given a hand *up*, not a hand*out*. The government should not reward laziness or other forms of irresponsibility. But even this allowed financial assistance should be administered on a state, and not federal level. It should be temporary and minimal. Welfare should be a temporary assistance which helps someone to get up off their feet, and it should be minimal as to not encourage the recipient to continue along their burdensome path while riding on the backs of others.

It is simply not the government's role in society to help those in need. That is the role of caring and compassionate individuals through private charity and of churches who will hopefully not only give the misfortunate the financial assistance they need, but the moral imagination to reverse a fundamental barrier to success: their lack of motivation.

Unfortunately, this *has* been the role the federal government has taken in the past half-century. President

First Principles for my First Election

Lyndon B. Johnson's began his "Great Society" program in the 1960's, which created an active role of the federal government to end poverty. When the welfare programs and other entitlements were implemented, only 4.3 million people were on the rolls. Now there are more than 40 million welfare recipients. I think it's safe to say that government isn't very effective in "ending poverty."[81]

However, in 1996 President Bill Clinton and a Republican controlled legislature made extraordinary progress in the effort to reduce poverty. But the fact was, they were not expanding the welfare system, but rather rolling it back. Welfare reform originated in the Republican principle that to put people back to work (self-reliance), rather than putting more and more of them on welfare checks was the most effective way to reduce poverty. It worked.

President Clinton grudgingly signed the welfare reform bill into law and the results are comforting:

"In 1996, the Aid to Families with Dependent Children (AFDC) program was transformed from a cash welfare program into a jobs program known as Temporary Assistance for Needy Families (TANF). Recipients were required to perform at least 20–30 hours per week of work or job preparation activities in exchange for the cash benefit.

Self Reliance

Overnight, welfare agencies became job placement offices, and people who had been trapped in poverty and dependence began seeking employment. Between 1996 and 2009, caseloads dropped from 4.5 million families to 1.7 million."[82]

The welfare reform bill of 1996 was a dramatic victory for the principle of self-reliance as it gave empirical evidence to the idea that reducing benefits and encouraging people to work, not giving them a handout, would be more beneficial in the long run. This is why it is not the federal government's job to bend to the whims of the irresponsible-it only further enslaves them to a life of poverty and mediocrity. The elected officials should continue to make common sense reforms, like that of the Republican 1996 reforms, which will foster an environment that rewards self-reliance and personal responsibility and promotes job growth.

The successes of the government policies in the 90's however, have been quickly compromised by the explosion of entitlements in the past decade. It is becoming clearer and clearer that no government policy, no matter how inventive will be able to remedy the dismal state of American affairs. It will take a revolution in the hearts and minds of the American people, especially of the Millennials, to turn this ship around. It will only be by the sheer power of the individual and the realigning of his conscience to restore America to its greatness. This change of

First Principles for my First Election

character must categorically condemn and oppose the temptation of victimization and dependency, and rather turn to the virtues of self-reliance and personal responsibility. To survive this crisis of debt and entitlement, we must make deliberate attempts in our own personal lives to live within our means and make wise financial decisions.

Naturally, all of us have different backgrounds and upbringings, and thus have different experience and different attitudes towards certain principles. In regards to the principle of self-reliance it's generally not a matter *if* people understand it, but *when* they begin to. I learned to appreciate the necessity of frugality and self-reliance at an early age. Unlike many, I learned the hard way. Of course there are thousands of kids across the country living in poverty that learned this principle more quickly than me. I've been blessed not to have experience that. But I have parents and grandparents who did. And it was their experiences that shaped my childhood, for the better I might add.

For the first 16 years of my life I wasn't allowed to spend a dime (that is until I had to buy a car). From early on my parents instilled me with an appreciation of thrift. All the money I received, be it from birthdays, Christmas, etc. was saved and locked away. I was never allowed to "waste" it on Pokémon cards or videogames. I never got to spend my money. In all honesty, if you would have asked me 10 years ago if I was a big advocate of thrift, my elementary school self probably would have replied

Self Reliance

first, "What's thrift?" and following the subsequent explanation, "NO WAY!"

In hindsight, I will do one thing that most teens and young adults (including myself) hate doing –admit my parents were right. Despite all the things that I always wish they'd done differently, I am glad that I wasn't allowed to spend my money. Over the years I've developed a conservative instinct to save. I save not only cash but change. Inspiring me to collect and save my change, was my step-dad who always had (and still does have) "The Big Jar." The big jar held his hundreds if not thousands of coins. It was where he would drop his day's change in when coming home from work. The jar, standing about two and a half to three feet tall, would routinely be dumped on to the floor and counted by my brother and me. After an hour or so of sifting, sorting, and counting, (my brother and I were always eager to find the newest state quarters or, if we were lucky, a wheat penny) we were constantly astounded at how much the change began to add up. What started as a jar full of change turned out to be a decent few hundred dollars! There is no doubt that these experiences strengthened my appreciation for thrift.

> "A penny saved is a penny earned!"
> –Benjamin Franklin

(Benjamin Franklin's saying comes to mind, "A penny saved is a penny earned!")

In my experience, the principles of thrift were taught to me by parental edict-no ands, ifs, or buts about it. But I also came to

First Principles for my First Election

appreciate the value of saving from the beloved tradition of emptying "the big jar." Parents have a responsibility of teaching these values to their children, and many tactics and strategies are employed. Not all kids grow up with the "save-your-money-thank-me-later" parents. Some kids learn the value of hard work through by their weekly allowances (and I mean allowances in the traditional sense of the term, referring to the time when actual chores were required to *earn* the money.). Personally, I never tasted of these blessings and was often told, "You work for food." Still others, I've learned, are required to reserve one third of the money for savings, one third for spending, and one third for church, as recommended by the financial guru Dave Ramsey. Regardless the method, understanding the principle of thrift is a necessity, and while it is certainly not impossible for adults to learn, it is best to be taught young.

Now however, our country is in a mess and too many people haven't learned the value of self-reliance. We, as Millennials, to kick it up a gear and start to pull ourselves up by our own boot straps. Becoming self-reliant won't be a walk in the park, nor will it be wildly popular or cool. It will mean making tough decisions. Maybe it will mean working part times while in school. Maybe it will mean not getting into hundreds of thousands of dollars into debt through student loans. Maybe it will mean learning to not live off our parents' backs.

Self Reliance

Whatever it means for you, I assure you that the long term benefits will be more than satisfying. The rewards of self-reliance are immeasurable. Independence! Freedom! And above all, the satisfaction of being your own person and living under your own roof by your own means. Security. Responsibility. Honest accomplishment. The only thing between that ultimate goal and you is motivation and a spirit of self-reliance. And in my opinion that is something we Millennials are far from lacking.

The overwhelming majority of Millennials enter their primitive adult life with a prideful spirit of individualism, self-confidence, and independence. We are ready to go to college (if not already there) and ready to live on our own, breaking free from the confines of our nest and soaring beyond the reach of our parents' protective wings. Bold, and sometimes brash, we are ready to take flight on our journey to the heights of the American Dream. We are filled to the brim with high hopes and expectations, savoring our newly won independence staring the world in the face. Fearless.

Furthermore, there is comfort in knowing that we are all Americans. What sets our nation apart is not our skin (there are many races among us), nor our religion (are we not as diverse?), it is our history and culture of principled individualism! We can make the tough decisions. We can right our wrongs. We can live within our means. And as much as we go through together, we take special pride in doing things ourselves, so that at the end of

First Principles for my First Election

the day the government is pushed aside and the rousing sprit of self-reliance stands. And with the enslaving monster of dependency slain, we can lift up our valiant and victorious chant so consistent with our history and heritage: "Yes, *I* can!"

Principle #5

American Exceptionalism

What's so great about America? According to some Millennials, not much.

While 80% of Americans in general view the United States as being an exceptional nation, [83][a] barely half (56%) of Millennials see it as so.[84] This statistic may come as a surprise to an older reader, but to a kid raised in the public school system, it comes as no surprise to me that nearly half of my generation lacks both respect and appreciation for our country. As thoroughly explained in the first chapter of this book, Intellectual Independence, the modern public education system has been hijacked by political activists who care more about indoctrinating the youth rather than teaching them. Among their political motivations is a constant

---

[a] Including 91% of Republicans, 77% of Independents, and only 73% of Democrats

First Principles for my First Election

flow of multiculturalist propaganda which distorts young people's perception of America.

This is accomplished both through blatant historical lies by liberal textbook oligopolists (Three K-12 textbook publishing companies capture about 85% of the market)[85b] and by the subtle diffusion of multiculturalist teaching methods. I have found that the problem has worsened since I have been through school. Twice, my younger brother has come home from elementary school singing songs of indoctrination in preparation for his class's music program. One such program revolved around the theme of global warming (a topic which I have already debunked). I credit the music teacher for her efforts, for the song was so catchy that even I remember the chorus: "It's getting hot down here/ we need to clean the air." The second program was around Christmas time. In this musical production all of the students in the fifth grade sang various holiday songs –Christmas songs, Jewish songs, and yes, even Kwanzaa songs.

It pains me to write the lyrics of the Kwanzaa song that I heard my brother singing –mainly because of how hilarious it was. Without actually hearing it, it's difficult for you, the reader, to understand how comical the school's attempt at diversity was. Accompanied by jungle-like African music, the students sang:

O Kwanzaa. O Kwanzaa.

---

[b] Similarly, five textbook publishing firms control about 80% of the college textbook market.

American Exceptionalism

O Kwanzaa. Kwanzaa.
O Kwanzaa. O Kwanzaa.
O Kwanzaa. Kwanzaa.

O Seven days of celebration.
Nguzo saba.
Seven days of celebration.
Habari gani?
Seven days of celebration.
Nguzo saba.
Seven days of celebration.
Harambee! (O)

O Kwanzaa. O Kwanzaa.
O Kwanzaa. Kwanzaa.
O Kwanzaa. O Kwanzaa.
O Kwanzaa. Kwanzaa.

O Seven days of celebration.
Nguzo saba.
Seven days of celebration.
Habari gani?
Seven days of celebration.
Nguzo saba.
Seven days of celebration.

First Principles for my First Election

Harambee! (O)

O Kwanzaa. O Kwanzaa.
O Kwanzaa. Kwanzaa.
O Kwanzaa. O Kwanzaa.
O Kwanzaa. Kwanzaa.
Harambee!

It's amazing to see how far schools will go just to give the appearance that they are tolerant and accepting of other cultures. But really, Kwanzaa? Has anybody explained to you the history behind this "holiday?" Kwanzaa is taught to students to be an ancient seven day celebration of seven traditional African values; however, it is actually an invented holiday created in the 1960s by radical Marxist and convicted felon Ron Karenga. Few remember that Karenga was sentenced to ten years in prison for his involvement in both murder and assault through his organization the United Slaves; rather, because of the public education system, we remember him for his mythical holiday of Kwanzaa. To give you a quick gist of what Kwanzaa is all about, two of the "traditional values" celebrated by Kwanzaa are the Marxist sounding principles of ujima and ujamma, or collective work and cooperative economics when translated from Swahili. This "holiday" has no historical, moral, or spiritual aspect. One magazine called it "a mishmash of different traditions and

American Exceptionalism

languages and blended them with Marxist ideas to reflect a unified African culture that doesn't exist anywhere."[86]

I'm not suggesting that the public school teachers at my brother's school are secretly trying to make all their students into Africa-worshipping, Marxist zombies. Most likely, the teachers themselves are ignorant of this history, however easy it is to find on the internet. My point, is that this is an example of how desperate public schools are to create the perceived atmosphere of cultural diversity. I suppose it gives them a feeling of moral elevation when they can fool themselves into thinking that they are teaching their students to understand the complexities of the world's many cultures. It is part of the common theme preached throughout the school system that America is just another country with just another culture. They tell us that there is nothing special about America –our traditions, our customs, our Judeo-Christian values, or our Western heritage. All cultures are inherently equal. Sometimes, they go as far to say that Western culture and the social and political institutions of the United States are inherently *inferior* to that of other cultures. These historical lies which falsely depict America's heritage as evil, violent, racist, and imperialistic are too numerous to unravel here. In fact, it will likely take an entire generation of historians to correct those distortions of our true noble heritage. However, if we are to restore the idea of American Exceptionalism, Millennials must seek out this history for ourselves. I will provide an intellectual

First Principles for my First Election

defense American Exceptionalism, outlining the origins and underpinnings of this idea, but I must leave it at that. For extensive arguments that refute the historical lies of the Left about our nation's heritage, I suggest further reading and investigation by the reader.[c]

The national attitude toward American Exceptionalism is beginning to shift largely due to the inability of conservatives articulate what it means for America to be "exceptional." Instead of a genuine and historically enriched opinion of American Exceptionalism, many young people see it as simply unfounded hubris and arrogant patriotism. Nationalism, the love of one's country, is considered the chiefest of sins among my generation and is a feeling thought to be held by the unenlightened in society who selfishly believe America to be superior to all other nations and cultures.

Unfortunately, my generation is not alone in these antagonistic feelings toward American patriotism and national pride. Shortly after his World Apology Tour in 2009,[d] President Obama himself echoed these sentiments when he famously quipped ""I believe in American Exceptionalism, just as I suspect

---

[c] *48 Liberal Lies about American History* by Larry Schweikart is a great start!
[d] Shortly after President Obama was inaugurated, he went on a tour of three continents in almost 100 days. Throughout this tour he gave numerous speeches in major world cities practically begging forgiveness and apologizing for the way the United States had treated the rest of the world. He apologized for our history, but especially for the War on Terror and the unwillingness of the Bush Administration to conform to internationalist initiatives such as global wealth redistribution and multilateral military action.

American Exceptionalism

that the Brits believe in British Exceptionalism and the Greeks believe in Greek Exceptionalism."[87] With these words President Obama displays the depth of his ignorance and the utter worthlessness of his Harvard education. I am ashamed that I have a president who has such contempt for this country and so perilously disrespects it using his world platform. We need a president who understands America and who can articulate its greatness.

What makes America exceptional is not our language, skin color, or any other demographic factor. Are we not significantly diverse in all of these areas? None of those things differentiates us from any other country. What does make America exceptional is our unique history. We are the only nation in the history of the world founded on the idea that man can govern himself. Ours was not a revolution of new ideas led by political radicals and reactionaries; the American Revolution was a restoration of old rights, the rights of Englishmen, and even older virtues, in the order of the Ancient Israelites from whom we derive our moral order. Ours was "not a revolution made, but prevented" as the great statesman Edmund Burke once declared. We are exceptional because of our unique structure of government ingeniously codified by our written Constitution. Throughout history Tyranny has proven to be the rule of human nature, Liberty is the exception. We are the exception.

First Principles for my First Election

While the idea of liberty is not necessarily new, its practical application certainly is. The history of man has been the history of slavery. Whether spiritually a slave to sin or politically a slave to government, it seems as if the condition of man on earth is one of oppression. It was not until the founding of the United States of America that man was given the opportunity to govern himself. Never before in the history of the world has a nation experienced the peace, stability, and prosperity in such a short length of time. In the mere 236 years since the birth of the Republic, our people have done more to advance the cause of liberty and prosperity than any other nation in the *thousands* of years of recorded human history.[e]

It wasn't an accident.

What was responsible for this unprecedented explosion of individual liberty, religious freedom, scientific innovation, and material prosperity? Was it our Constitution? Yes...and no.

Our Constitution was a work of genius. Its framers included James Madison, Benjamin Franklin, George Washington, and Alexander Hamilton among other recognizable names in American history. All together 55 delegates, each man representing his own state, attended the Constitutional Convention in Philadelphia to create the Union we know today.[f] Thomas

---

[e] I recommend reading *The 5,000 Year Leap* by W. Cleon Skousen; this is one of my favorite books and through its discussion of first principles, it helped me to grasp how drastically America changed the course of human history.

[f] Note that 39 of the 55 delegates actually signed the Constitution.

American Exceptionalism

Jefferson, who was in France during the Constitutional Convention, called them an "assembly of demigods" for their degree of high intellect and profound moral courage. [88] Young, wealthy, and educated, this convention of statesmen possessed perhaps the greatest collective wisdom about history, political structures, and economic systems in the world. Learned in both religion and the classics, they understood the governing forces behind civilization allowing them to construct a government that would endure the test of time and defend against the wild infatuations of human nature.

James Madison, the "father of the Constitution," certainly knew a thing or two about theses complex issues. Displaying extreme dedication and disciplined diligence, Madison wrote a letter to his friend Thomas Jefferson (who was in Paris at the time) to send him over from Europe every book on history and political philosophy that he could find. Jefferson honored Madison's request, and throughout the spring and summer of 1786 leading up to the Constitutional Convention Madison buried himself in his books. Desperately wishing to craft a proper form of government for the American people, he carefully noted the strengths and weaknesses of different political structures. He noted the reasons for the successes and failures of empires. He studied the moral order of the Ancient Israelites, the follies of Greek democracy, and the rise and fall of the Roman Republic.

First Principles for my First Election

Finally, he published his *Notes on Ancient and Modern Confederacies* which detailed his findings.[89]

Madison and other founders such as John Jay and Alexander Hamilton also wrote a series of publications known as *The Federalist Papers* which proved to be an exhaustive intellectual defense of the new Constitution and which successfully secured the popular support of New York and Pennsylvania to the cause of Union. In *Federalist #51*, Madison shows that his intensive study of history paid off, as he brilliantly articulates the importance of our unique and truly exceptional form of government:

"But what is government itself, but the greatest of all reflections on human nature? If men were angels, no government would be necessary. If angels were to govern men, neither external nor internal controls on government would be necessary. In framing a government which is to be administered by men over men, the great difficulty lies in this: you must first enable the government to control the governed; and in the next place oblige it to control itself. A dependence on the people is, no doubt, the primary control on the government; but experience has taught mankind the necessity of auxiliary precautions."[90]

Ultimately, Madison says, government is a reflection and a response to the evils of human nature. All his studies of history

American Exceptionalism

seemed to point him in the direction of devising a government with every possible check against power and centralization –both against the nation's citizens and their leaders.

Russell Kirk echoes this thought more succinctly. "Man being complex, his government cannot be simple."[91] The Founders understood the complexity of man's natural condition. Man is naturally corruptible and fallible. He can and will make mistakes. In positions of authority, he will abuse his power. The founders distrusted the concentration of political authority in the hands of one or even a few individuals; but however much they feared the restoration of a monarchy, they detested the tyranny of the majority even more. The educated statesmen knew their history. They had read about Greece and the dangers of democracy unchecked and unrestrained. Their aristocratic position in society led them to fear what Alexander Tocqueville came to call "democratic despotism" –rule by the masses without respect to minority rights and privileges. The Founders didn't want a democracy; they wanted a republic. To those ends, they looked to the roots and inner workings of the Ancient Roman Republic. Not only did the founders create a federal government –in which power and authority is divided between the national government and the states- but they also instituted a separation of powers between the three branches, a practice advocated by the Enlightenment philosopher Montesquieu in his *Spirit of the Laws*. The Legislative, Executive, and Judicial branches of the federal

First Principles for my First Election

government were created to be coequal and able to check the other's power. All of these measures and precautions (and so many others) were set into place so that power would never be concentrated in either the hands of a tyrant or the unbridled masses. This combination of political contrivances was the culmination of thousands of years of history. The seed of Western civilization and our American Order was planted long ago; it simply came to bloom under the care and direction of these American patriots.

Our Constitution truly was organic. It grew within the context of our own nation's history and therefore has certain characteristics that are uniquely American. Though the 55 gentleman that met during those summer months of 1787 were all educated and morally upstanding, all had different ideas and different interests. As delegates of their states, they had to advocate a system that their own people could support. Therefore, out of a web of contradicting interests between the big states and small states, federalists and anti-federalists, abolitionists and slavery-advocates, our Constitution was born in a bundle of compromises. Out of it came a uniquely bicameral legislature; the House which would represent the people (its proportional allocation of delegates would inevitably favor bigger states) and the Senate which would represent the states (equal representation would favor smaller states).[g] A Bill of Rights was added to

---

[g] During the time that the Constitution was crafted, Senators were not elected

American Exceptionalism

appease a strong anti-federalist movement via the first ten amendments; and the 3/5 compromise and the ban on the importation of slaves featured the first steps toward a nation which would eventually abolish slavery.

No other country can claim the republican form of government that we enjoy today. No other country been able to reconcile the diversity and differences of its people through such creative compromises. Finally, no other nation can claim such a remarkable group of educated and moral men who have led them forward successfully in the quest for ordered liberty. The ingenious framers, complex structure, and organic development of our Constitution are without a doubt exceptional.

Is the American Constitution the only source of our freedom and prosperity? Not necessarily. Today in the 21st century, countless countries around the world operate under some sort of constitution (though none can claim one exactly the same as our own). France, Germany, and Great Britain all have constitutions. Even the former Soviet Union had a constitution and a Bill of Rights much more extensive than ours! So does that make these countries, past or present, more free? Absolutely not! It surely didn't turn out too well for the Soviets...

Why has the American Constitution been so much more successful in maintaining order and internal stability as well as

---

by the people, but rather by state legislators, thus empowering the states even further.

First Principles for my First Election

religious and civil liberty for its citizens? I think the answer can be summarized by my favorite author Russell Kirk, who states in *The Conservative Mind*, that "Liberty is not to be got by simple proclamation; it is the creation of civilization and of heroic exertions by a few brave souls."[92] Later, he reiterates this point saying, "Liberty is a product of civilization and a reward of virtue."[93] Simply put, paper can't give you liberty any more than government can. Liberty cannot simply be proclaimed. It must grow. It requires an environment and culture that respects morality and a society whose laws conform to natural law. True liberty requires a people dedicated to virtuous self-restraint; otherwise the law will be impotent to protect either their lives or property. Liberty requires a communal faith in institutions higher than the individual. It requires faith in God, in the church, in the rule of law, in tradition, in custom –all the natural defenses against the human appetite for destruction.

These things the United States had, and to some extent still do have. These are the things which make America exceptional. The ingenious crafting of the Constitution gave us a firm foundation and a society structure within to work, but it is the moral fabric of our nation which truly holds us together.

Today we still reap the fruits of economic prosperity and moral stability from the generous seeds sown by our Founders. Though the radical forces of industrialization and postmodern culture unceasingly attack the traditional values and ideas that

American Exceptionalism

made this country exceptional, there is a resurgence of conservative thought that is constructing a valiant defense against them. Though we are now a minority, the strength and durability of our institutions have left individuals such as myself a pathway to pursue the truth and to defend liberty. Faith in our republican system of government –with the separation of power, checks and balances, and states' rights- remains strong. The Church, though weakened by the powers of secularism, remains active and alive in the United States and serves as a sanctuary for souls, both young and old, who desire a purpose in life greater than material satisfaction. The strength our collective institutions, both political and social, is what makes the character of our nation's individuals exceptional.

Stories of *individual* exceptionalism in the United States abound because of the opportunity for economic and spiritual growth offered within these borders. I have already given accounts of my family's life stories in the Self-Reliance chapter to show how the American Dream is still alive (though it is under attack by the current administration). However, I believe that those who can teach us the most about the exceptional nature of American society are those who are foreign to it.

Kevin Okseniuk was the salutatorian of my graduating high school class. Born and raised in Buenos Aires, Argentina, he lived in poverty as the son of a preacher until his family moved to the States when he was in eighth grade; he could not speak a word

First Principles for my First Election

of English. Five years later he found himself graduating second in our class of 464 students in one of the most academically competitive counties in the state of Tennessee. He now attends Georgia Tech, one of the most prestigious engineering colleges in the nation, on a full-ride scholarship.

During his passionate and moving salutatorian speech, Kevin gave an account of how much he had accomplished in the short time that he had been in the country. Despite his rough beginnings as the "Magnet school reject" (a term he applied to himself after being denied admission into a County Engineering Magnet School shortly after he moved to New Jersey), Kevin was able to excel in nearly every field to which he applied himself. His initial bitterness and disappointment quickly transformed into immense appreciation and gratitude towards his new country.

"Reflecting on our past is never easy," he said. "There is a constant tension between the memories we want to let go and cannot, and the memories that we would like to hang onto forever but life forces us to leave behind...We can all look at our past in different ways. I believe that gratitude is the most helpful of them. I also believe it is the most natural and rational of our responses, because time moves forward and gratitude is the only way of looking back in time that adds to the value of the present and the future. It is, perhaps, the most wise, for only a foolish person could claim that he has achieved everything on his own."

American Exceptionalism

He proceeded to express his gratitude for all who had personally touched his life and encouraged him along the way, thanking his friends, teachers, administrators, and of course, his beloved country for giving him the opportunity to succeed.

"I'm grateful for the United States of America and for the values that govern this land. Although I was born and raised in another country, I have come to adopt America as my own home. As a child growing up watching translated American movies and reading articles about this culture, I never truly understood why Americans were so proud of their homeland –now I do…and, friends, trust me, you have the most valid of reasons and plenty of evidence to back it up. Freedom works. We are blessed to live in a country that dignifies hard work and respect for others –and I'm a product of that."

Naturally, the audience erupted in applause. At the end of his address, Kevin received a standing ovation that warmed my heart and wet more than a few eyes, including my mom's. As a close personal friend, Kevin had been over to my house more than a few times; He loved my mom's good southern cooking! All that to say, my family and I loved him and cherished his friendship. We knew how much he had been through and how much this experience meant to him.

First Principles for my First Election

Though there may be Millennials who refuse to acknowledge, out of ignorance or hate, our nation's unique and providentially-inspired history I do not see how anyone could look at Kevin's story and not see that America is truly exceptional. Of course, Kevin was not guaranteed success or destined for greatness simply because he landed on the American shores and applied for citizenship. His academic success came with the rich *opportunity* that we enjoy in this great country. Our culture, our society, and our political institutions are structured to allow individuals the opportunity to achieve their maximum potential.

Kevin took advantage of those opportunities and societal benefits, but his individual dedication and perseverance cannot be understated. His determination to master the English language also cannot be overlooked. As he states in his salutatorian speech, Kevin spent hours in the public library translating children's books from Spanish into English. What must have been a humiliating experience for any other eighth grader, Kevin turned into a valuable exercise in assimilation. All his hard work and dedication paid off. Though he tends to shy away from politics, I understand that he is inwardly a strong proponent of making English the official language of the United States and requiring immigrants to make an effort to assimilate in that respect –not because he thinks that English is inherently superior to any other language (he still speaks Spanish at home), but because he understands how influential it was in his assimilation to a new

American Exceptionalism

land and new culture, enabling him to adapt and succeed in whatever he decided to pursue.

Ironically, Millennials tend to get uncomfortable with public policies that promote national unity and social cohesion, such as making English the official language. Too many seem to perceive these policies as being racist or anti-immigrant, as if promoting political and cultural unity somehow trespasses on their sacred principles of diversity and tolerance. In this area of public policy, it is clear that Millennials have been taken captive by the multiculturalist doctrines preached by self-righteous academics on the Left who value their own self-esteem more than their own national heritage. I suppose it makes people feel good when they can convince themselves that they are defending poor, helpless immigrants from the racist and evil schemes of mean-spirited conservatives. However, immigration policies that promote national and social cohesion are the greatest supports to the immigrant community. Language, as Kevin so completely understands, provides a medium for the seamless communication and free exchange of ideas that any free society requires for its well-being and self-preservation. These policies are the greatest sources of opportunity for immigrants who truly are poor and helpless. These requirements and regulations are designed to lift them up out of poverty and to usher them into the civil society which American citizens enjoy. Among the questions that Mark Levin raises in his book *Liberty and Tyranny* are, "How can the

First Principles for my First Election

alien participate fully in American society if he does not share the language that binds citizen to citizen? How can he acquire better skills, pursue higher learning, or interact effectively in the marketplace if he does not speak English…and most importantly, how can the alien comprehend the nation's founding principles and pledge allegiance to them if he cannot be sure of their intended meaning?"[94] Don't take it from me –or Mark Levin; take it from my good friend Kevin and the countless immigrants who have learned the language and made a name for themselves and their families in these great United States.

I have also had the pleasure of coming to know Galina Koval, a refugee from the former Soviet Union. In my earlier chapter "Intellectual Independence," I explain how I met her at my church and read her revealing autobiography *From Darkness to Great Light*. I also discussed her terrible experience in the institutions of higher education in the Soviet Empire, which she called "ideological institutions" –an expression I find eerily fitting for our devolving American universities. Here I have reserved a few moments to discuss her profound appreciation and respect for America once again.

Whether on college campuses or on the front lines of the Occupy protests, Millennials have increasingly begun to toy with leftist philosophies such as socialism and communism in recent years. Though most young people are not politically educated or engaged, most see the radical philosophies of socialism and

American Exceptionalism

communism as at least well-intentioned, and they are generally accepted as legitimate political theories. Some slack must be granted, however, for the blatant ignorance and naiveté of my generation. Historically speaking, younger generations are more receptive to radical thinking and susceptible to political demagoguery. It is for this very reason that Galina Koval has been an outspoken advocate for American exceptionalism, and has valiantly taken to the war of ideas to combat the oppressive thinking of the regime from which she escaped.

Galina Koval saw firsthand the horrors of communism and the effects social leveling policies in the Soviet Union. It was this firsthand, behind the scenes experience that gave her immense gratitude and appreciation for the political and moral stability in the United States. She saw firsthand how the destruction of private property led to the demolition of wealth, initiative, creativity, and industry. She saw the government attacks upon the wealthy, the inventors, and the intellectuals. She saw the inevitable consequences of "spreading the wealth around." She experienced food lines. She experienced communal housing, in which she and her daughter were forced for a time to live with complete strangers (including many thieves and criminals) in a tiny government operated apartment. She saw the effects of a society deprived of religion, and whose moral compass (or lack thereof) was directed by the State. She saw the effects of drunkenness, thievery, and a general lack of trust or faith in community. All of

First Principles for my First Election

these things Mrs. Koval experienced and forcibly endured until she was finally able to escape to America.

Once she arrived she was overwhelmed by the culture shock. In her book she recounts the story of her first visit to an American supermarket, where she nearly fainted over how many fresh bananas they had at a single store (bananas are her favorite fruit). In general she was astounded by the amount of wealth and economic opportunity to be found in this new country. The Soviet state-controlled media had deceived her and the rest of her countrymen about the condition of the "evil, capitalist" United States, which they believed to be in worse shape than their own. Mrs. Koval came to understand that the political and economic liberty of the United States was the reason for its unmatched prosperity.

She quickly realized, however, that there was more to America's exceptionalism than its material abundance. Almost immediately, she realized that there was something intrinsically different about the people themselves that differentiated the United States from her home in the Soviet Empire. She found that public virtue and generosity were nearly as abundant in this new country as were bananas! Mrs. Koval chronicles how she and her fellow countrymen developed a sense of distrust and skepticism of other people after living under the harsh conditions of Soviet social life. She found, however, that this level of distrust was not necessary in America. People were generally kind, benevolent,

American Exceptionalism

and sober rather than mean, malevolent, and drunk. Mrs. Koval concluded that what made this huge difference was the presence and influence of Christianity in the United States.

Galina Koval had been raised an atheist –not only did her parents lack religious conviction, but her own country, the Soviet Union, did as much as it could to institutionalize atheism as a sort of state religion. The Soviet government, proud of its extensive bill of rights, (as mentioned earlier) boasted of its policy of religious toleration. However, as her autobiography discloses, only a few of the old orthodox churches in the Soviet Empire were allowed by the government to function. Mrs. Koval states very plainly that they were orchestrated by the KGB in order to ensure that they did not become too powerful or turn into centers of dissent. "Candidates to the priesthood had to be approved by a special department of the government…without showing a passport, a person could not be baptized, or arrange a wedding or funeral ceremony. All these events had to be reported to the KGB, and participants risked their careers and the future of their children." Her one visit to one of the orthodox churches was awkward and confusing. All the proceedings were conducted in an old Slav language, so she could not understand what was being said. Nothing was explained to accommodate visitors. Furthermore, she was confused by the outlandish respect that people gave to statues and other "holy" artifacts.

First Principles for my First Election

Even as a university professor, Mrs. Koval was prohibited from learning about religion, let alone Christianity. However, the Soviet government –conscious that the learned professors of their state-run universities would likely wonder and seek out answers about religion for themselves- provided a class for the educators that instructed them on what they wanted them to know about the subject. Mrs. Koval writes that she and other educators were told a few details about major world religions, but not the whole story. The basic purpose of the class, though, was to denigrate Christianity and the other world religions, reducing them to the same status as Greek mythology. That was the only experience Mrs. Koval was permitted to have in her world of material and spiritual darkness.

Upon arriving in the United States, Mrs. Koval was taken in by a New Jersey family that she had once met in the Soviet Union. This family became the first to introduce Mrs. Koval to true religion. She attended a church of Christ in New Jersey and was delighted with what she found. She began to study the Bible for herself and attended every Bible class and church service that she could in order to learn more about the faith. What convicted her heart the most, however, was the amazing character and hospitality that her Christian friends showed her. She was mesmerized by their example, and the more she learned about Christianity and its Christian followers, the more she was

American Exceptionalism

convinced that America's *material* success was founded in *religious* conviction.

Galina Koval's story illustrates in a beautiful way the transformative power of faith in the community. Her life is a testament to the fact that a free society cannot exist in a political and economic vacuum —where the individual is divorced from his religious context and devoid of his moral obligations. The Soviets extended the Left's doctrine of social, political, and economic equality to its natural conclusion; their socio-economic experiment was a travesty to humanity and ended with the deaths of millions. Millennials would be wise to stay clear of such radical thinking and outright dangerous philosophies. We are not immune from such moral and political destruction simply because we are Americans. There is nothing significant about our title, nothing magical about our blood. What makes us exceptional, what gives us the slightest hope that we can sustain the flame of liberty for generations to come, is our history. A unique constitution, a rich set of political traditions, and a multitude of God-fearing people unite us under Old Glory. Those things we must maintain. Those things we must restore.

Throughout this book I have laid out solutions for how my generation, the Millennials, might start a counter-culture movement to restore the virtues outlined above —how we might combat the foes of liberty on the domestic front by resurrecting our moral imagination, restoring our traditions, and engaging in

First Principles for my First Election

the war of ideas. But the passage above begs the question: How are we as Americans to defend this exceptional nation from enemies abroad?

It doesn't take a Ph.D. in foreign affairs to realize that the world has become more dangerous than anytime in recorded history. Revolutions have ignited the Middle East and seem to spread like wildfire. Nuclear weapons and other weapons of mass destruction have become household goods for most developed countries, including unstable regimes such as Pakistan, North Korea, and Russia.[95h] Cyber terrorism is quickly becoming an increasingly silent and invisible but all too deadly threat. Islamic extremism continues to threaten civil and religious liberty across the globe, and economic instability due to irresponsible fiscal policies have constructed a house of cards that could topple and send the world into a dastardly depression at the drop of a hat.

There is no advantage what-so-ever in ignoring these somber facts. It will do no good for Millennials to pretend that the revolutions in the Middle East are simply organic movements for a tolerant and peaceful democracy. It will do no good for Millennials to fantasize about world peace through the proliferation of nuclear weapons. It will do no good for Millennials to pretend that cyber threats will just go away. And

---

[h] The country of Iran, run by radical Islamists, is closer than ever to developing a nuclear weapon as it continues to enrich its supply of uranium, rebel against economic sanctions, and impede international peace-keeping negotiations.

American Exceptionalism

for all things good and holy, it would be a shame to make believe that 9/11 didn't happen.

Now is not the time for childish political games when it comes to American foreign policy. Now is the time, more than ever, to have a focused and *principled* foreign policy. I believe the best principled approach to foreign relations was articulated by the great statesman and President Ronald Reagan who called for the prudent policy of "peace through strength." This principled approach to foreign policy successfully carried us through nearly two decades of peace and prosperity. With it we defeated the Soviet Union, which Reagan called an "Evil Empire," without setting the world on fire. Though we did engage in a nuclear arms race, it was our superiority in strength that kept the peace. All this success started with the simple notion that the military must be priority number one for the federal government.

Ronald Reagan understood the necessity for government to "provide for the common defense," as required by the Constitution. Like the founders, he knew that the security of life, liberty, and property was the primary purpose of government and one of the few things that is best achieved collectively rather than individually. Too often, our representatives get lost in their own pride and arrogance and forget the true purpose of government. It is not to develop into a Nanny State, where the State supplies our every want and need; the purpose of government is to provide for the common defense.

First Principles for my First Election

Not all of our elected officials have their priorities straight, and consequently one of the biggest threats to our nation's military comes from within. Defense spending is being gutted by Leftist politicians who apparently care more about government handouts than national security. Defense spending comprises only 20% of the federal budget (even though it is the primary purpose of government), while entitlements make up nearly two thirds.[96] Under the administration of President Obama, that number is falling even greater. "Since President Obama took office, more than 50 major weapons programs at a value of more than $300 billion were cut or delayed. On top of this, the Administration told the military to cut almost $600 billion more over the next 15 years."[97] The Navy is the smallest it has been since 1916; and due to the "NEW START" treaty that President Obama signed with the Russians, the United States has been forced to dramatically decrease our supply of nuclear warheads, while Russia maintains a 10:1 tactical-nuclear weapons advantage.[98][99]

In addition, the missile defense program –a project started by President Reagan- is being drastically cut. The U.S. government has the technology to destroy a nuclear weapon in mid-flight high above the atmosphere so that it does not harm inhabitants below. This technology is very advanced, but also very expensive. Since we only have limited access to it, the technology is primarily used to protect areas of high population concentration in the United States. Historically, however, we have also used this

American Exceptionalism

technology as a sort of "nuclear umbrella" for other parts of the world. Past administrations have negotiated with foreign governments who have promised not to develop nuclear weapons of their own if we (the United States) will protect them with our missile defense technology. Thus, this program has done wonders to reduce the number of nuclear warheads world-wide. President Obama stopped that progress dead in its tracks. In 2009, President Obama abruptly abandoned America's commitment to place land-based interceptors in Poland and a radar in the Czech Republic, while simultaneously docking the missile defense budget 16%.[100]

The security of our country is being severely threatened by our own politicians who have neglected their constitutional obligation to provide for the common defense. While I have passionately supported spending cuts elsewhere in this book, on principle Millennials must understand that defense should not be the first place we go to look for budget gutting. Yes, we could achieve some savings by making defense contracts more efficient, and we could save money by avoiding unnecessary military conflicts (such as our involvement in Egypt and Libya), but these are only minimal savings compared to how much money can be salvaged through entitlement reform.

Neither does giving priority to military spending and activities mean that we should seek to become an aggressive and imperial power. Such motivations would surely taint the private and public purity of our self-acclaimed American exceptionalism.

First Principles for my First Election

On the contrary, a "peace through strength" foreign policy is a purely defensive strategy of self-preservation that exercises the most extreme caution and prudence; it is a strategy hesitant to involve our nation in affairs that do not concern us and it is resistant to imperialistic expansion. While it is true that our country has had spurts of expansionist fervor, we have largely been of an isolationist mindset and unorthodoxly self-controlled as a world superpower when put in proper historical context. We have hardly been the evil, greedy land-grubbers that revisionist historians have depicted the United States.

Early on in our Republic's history George Washington, in his farewell address, urged the newborn country to "avoid entangling alliances" and to steer clear of European conflicts and rivalries. While he did not advocate complete and unconditional neutrality in foreign affairs, President Washington knew that the new country –still defining its political identity and recovering its economic health from a hard fought Revolution- could not afford another war anytime soon. The nation needed time to recover and rebuild. Prudence and patience were his policies. Peace through strength.

Even the more radical and daring Thomas Jefferson, who was a strong advocate of supporting the French Revolution militarily earlier in his life, later concluded that "We are friends of liberty everywhere, [but] custodians only of our own." This statement shows that Jefferson proved to be a much more

American Exceptionalism

moderate President than a philosopher. (The feeling of responsibility truly is a transformative power!) Contrary to popular opinion, however, Jefferson was no pacifist. When America's interests were directly threatened, he responded swiftly and strongly.

A group of Muslim extremists known as the Barbary Pirates (located off the coast of Tripoli in Africa) had pestered the American government since its birth.[101i] The pirates regularly looted American trade ships and forced the American government to pay extortion for the return of captured citizens. As a newly formed nation the country was too weak militarily to defend itself against these pesky pirates; they were forced to pay the bounty. Eventually, the pirates overstepped their bounds to the point that President Thomas Jefferson was forced to respond. In a well calculated and well-orchestrated attack, the American government deployed a group of Marines to eliminate the pirate problem once and for all. Thus began the American legacy of self-preservation from all enemies, foreign or domestic. Since that battle over 200 years ago our nation has proved fully competent to defend herself and hold her own in the world.

Most Millennials (and most Americans) would admit that the intricate complexities and complicated workings of foreign

---

[i] Isn't it ironic that the first country to declare war on the United States after winning independence was the Muslim nation of Tripoli? Most Americans haven't even heard of the conflict that began in 1801 and lasted through four presidencies. The "war on terror" is nearly as old as America herself!

First Principles for my First Election

affairs are the furthest things from their minds –as they should be. We should not overly concern ourselves with things that we cannot directly control. Our energies should be focused on the renewal and regeneration of intellectual and spiritual growth as well as the restoration of financial responsibility in our private and public lives. If these things, says Dr. Russell Kirk, "can be satisfied with reasonable success, then the problems of war and peace are likely to fall into some manner of settlement, so far as the issues of war and peace can ever be settled among men." Matters of war –"the conundrum of atomic energy and new weapons of war, the success or failure of international organizations…these are not problems for the conservative thought, or radical thought either, strictly speaking: they are problems of expediency, to be met by the soldier and the diplomat."[102] Millennials need not get tied down in the details of foreign relations. This is one area of government from which the founders wanted to shield the public. Difficult military decisions and strategies that could involve the deaths of millions should not be up for popular vote, those are decisions to be made by elected officials and experienced military officers whom we trust. The best thing Americans, and Millennials, could do on that front is to be charitable and hospitable to the armed forces. We should never underestimate the power of our patriotism in supporting the morale of the brave men and women who are daily prepared to make the ultimate sacrifice for our freedom. There is special

American Exceptionalism

nobility, also, in the completely voluntary enlistment of the armed service.

I'm sure that Dr. Kirk would agree, however, that since the Obama administration has so drastically politicized our nation's military endeavors it has become more imperative than ever to rediscover the first principles of national defense. I refute, and encourage Millennials to reject, the foreign policies of the Obama administration not simply because of differences in opinion or strategy, but because they have consistently proven to be nothing more than a systematic deconstruction of the finest military in the world.

Not only has President Obama defunded and undersupplied the military, but he has also misdirected its resources and exploited it for political ends. He undermined the leadership of our most experienced military officers when he single-handedly set the level of troop withdrawal from forces in Afghanistan. Without the constitutionally required consent of Congress –a formal declaration of war- he recklessly involved U.S. forces in two additional world conflicts –Egypt and Libya.

In the name of "freedom" and "democracy" our government supported a revolution that toppled a regime friendly to the United States and tolerant towards Israel, albeit oppressive to its own people. Now that the Egyptian people have toppled their government, they have elected radical Islamic extremist, Mohamed Morsi, a member of the Muslim Brotherhood to be their

First Principles for my First Election

new president. The Muslim Brotherhood was founded by Egyptian radicals in 1928 who sought to overthrow monarchy, expel Western forces, and establish Islamic law worldwide.[103][j] Now, the radical group has won the presidency. In the words of one commentator, *"That's* what democracy looks like" in the Middle East –one radical for another.

In Libya, President Obama also lent revolutionary radicals the credibility and military support of the United States. The Libyans have assassinated their leader Quadaffi and are in the process of restructuring their government. Largely a tribal people, many observers think that it will be difficult for them to construct a working government at all.[104] So what have we received in return? More chaos and more instability.

President Obama seems perfectly content to defund and destabilize the nation's military. On the rare occasions when he does exercise his authority as commander in chief, it is when he can benefit politically here at home. So long as he can convince the ignorant masses and idealistic Millennials that he is fighting for "freedom," he is sure to score political points. Make no mistake: throughout this election cycle President Obama is sure to tout the "successes" of his needless foreign excursions and dangerous adventures. Even in these military ventures, the President has surrendered to the Will of the "international

---

[j] The group's motto is "Allah is our objective. The Prophet is our leader. Koran is our law. Jihad is our way. Dying in the way of Allah is our highest hope."

American Exceptionalism

community." He refuses to lead and willingly makes our nation obedient to the Will and General Interest of international organizations like the United Nations. The President of the United States has more power than any other individual on the face of the globe, and historically he has been the leader of the free world. On that front, President Obama has been an abject failure.

Moderate Millennials made find my forthright condemnation of the President and his party's foreign policy startling. Some might be wondering what motive the President could have, other than political expediency, which could enable his conscious to justify such military failures and allow such world catastrophes. If one is willing to look at history and accept its lessons, I think the answer is rather simple.

Since the days of Woodrow Wilson, the Left has had a history of sacrificing America's interest upon the altar of the General Will in hopes of someday achieving the fantasy of what they call "world peace."[k] Whether through reckless isolation, needless intervention, or mindless subservience to the international community, the Left nearly always takes the wrong side in foreign affairs. This drastic difference is no matter of

---

[k] Woodrow Wilson proposed the idea of a "League of Nations" after the end of WWI in hopes for securing something close to world peace. Isolationist Republicans in Congress never agreed to the treaty, so the United States never entered the international organization. The League proved useless in preventing Hitler from coming to power and all the disasters during WWII that he inflicted. Nevertheless, the League was the inspiration for the United Nations, of which the United States is now a part.

First Principles for my First Election

policy; it is a matter of principle. It is the result of a world view that detests American exceptionalism.

For nearly a century, the American Left has been rooted in the idea that there is nothing exceptional about America. They have been spoon-fed the lies propagated by liberal academics that there is nothing providential about our country's historical conception, nothing unique about its government, and nothing noble about its people. Some, even our own President on his World Apology Tour, have suggested that America has been a nuisance to the world, as if we are nothing more than arrogant, selfish, capitalist pigs. Once Millennials are able to see past the haze put in front of them by liberal educators, once they are able to break out of that intellectual and moral conformity imposed by our mass culture, and once they can get inside the mind of a true believer, it is easy to see how so many on the Left justify the systematic degeneration of America as a world super power. Only a self-loathing and bitter indignation towards America could inspire support for the anti-patriotic measures which so dangerously threaten her freedom, security, and sovereignty.[1]

I propose no specific alternative to the strategy we should take in foreign policy. Such an action would be foolish and would

---

[1] In *Roots of Obama's Rage*, author Dinesh D'Souza explores the President's rich history of anti-colonialism, which he suggests is rooted in his family's history of resistance to imperial Britain and western democracies. Much of D'Souza's conclusions are drawn from Obama's own autobiography, *Dreams from my Father*, in which he chronicles his Kenyan father's history of resistance to "evil" western democracies.

American Exceptionalism

only prove my youthful naiveté. As I have continually stated throughout this book, this Millennial's Manifesto is about principles, not politics. The *principles* which I believe must guide our foreign policy must be founded in the steadfast belief that America is exceptional and that her sovereignty must be adequately defended so that she may remain a bastion of freedom for her inhabitants and a shining example to the world. If Millennials want the security and the peace of mind necessary to enjoy the fruits of a civil society –if we want to keep the American Dream alive for our generation- we must vote for leaders who will exercise prudence, caution, and careful consideration to each military decision. Only men who have the courage, honor, and wisdom to see the world as it is will be able to establish a lasting peace. As articulated by that great thinker Dr. Kirk,

"An intelligent conservative feels that the ills of the world cannot be cured by any single ingenious system of improvisation or any solemn political contrivance. Each problem must be considered upon its own terms, but in the light of the wisdom of our ancestors."[105]

Principle #6

Civic Duty

"We have heard enough of liberty and the rights of man; it is high time to hear something of the duties of men and the rights of authority."[106]

Millennials, like most Americans, are easily swayed by language. Words like "liberty" and "social justice" are tickling to our ears, but we instinctively perceive words like "duty" and "responsibility" as repulsive. It may be human nature to react in such a way. Since creation man has been in a state of rebellion against Authority –rebellion against God and all earthly established order. Man wishes to be the master of his own fate and the keeper of his own soul; he is impulsively lawless. History, however, has proven that man actually thrives when liberty is

First Principles for my First Election

under law and benefits when man is obedient to order and submissive to authority, legitimate authority that is.

It may be fun and convenient to think ourselves born as completely free and autonomous individuals, but as I have repeatedly demonstrated throughout this book, that is not the case. We are all born into this world totally helpless, (physically and spiritually) completely dependent on our family and on our community for survival. Indeed we thrive when placed in the context of community and in the loving fellowship of others. We need relationships. We need the church. We need order. Law itself is meant to be liberating (though this may seem paradoxical to our modern minds). Out of this community of individuals, out of this order we develop a sense of belonging to the society from which we came. Out of this sense of belonging originates certain duties and responsibilities necessary for the maintenance and preservation of civil society. This is not to say that everything that we become in our lives is all to the credit of some amorphous mass with whom you can't identify. Nor is this to say that our duties and responsibilities *solely* involve "giving back" to society.

When I speak of duties and responsibilities, I am talking about the necessity for all individuals to become self-reliant and independent. I am talking about the need for an individual to earn a living and then to faithfully contribute to those institutions which continue to support him. In this country we also have the privilege, the honor, to participate in our own government so that

Civic Duty

our best interests are served and our financial contributions are not abused. That means we have a duty to move out of our parents' houses. We have a duty to provide for ourselves, our families, our churches, and our government. Finally, we have a responsibility to take part in it all through the glorious process of self-government. Enough talk, indeed, about our "rights" and our precious "liberties!" Enough about what we think we are entitled to and enough of what we want from others! In the words of JFK, "Ask not what your country can do for you; ask what you can do for your country."

Engaging in the public discourse and getting involved in the community shouldn't be like pulling teeth. Our "duty" to be involved in society should really be looked upon as an *honor*. Early in our Republic's history, this was the case. Americans were a ragtag group of people –mostly farmers- who had miraculously thrown off the yoke of slavery from the largest Empire in the world. They did not have trouble looking for reasons to participate in self-government. Revolutionary patriot Samuel Adams said that "at the moment [each citizen] is offering his vote…he is executing one of the most solemn trusts in human society for which he is accountable to God and his country." The passion of Mr. Adams is apparent and the love he displays for his country and its mode of self-government is even more heart-warming.

Unfortunately Millennials and many other Americans have turned that "solemn trust" into a burdensome chore. In the worst

First Principles for my First Election

of cases, voting is entirely neglected. *It's too much trouble...I don't have time....My vote doesn't count...I don't even care*, are all common excuses. At the very best, voting is just another checklist item around election time and not a truly valued American tradition.

Naturally, voter turnout rates fluctuate over the years depending on the times and which hot-button issues dominate the age. Due to the "historic nature" of the 2008 election, voter turnout reached a record 65% -a percentage not achieved since 1960.[a] This was obviously an anomaly, considering that in an average election, the percentage of Americans who vote is closer to 50%. This abandonment of duty and responsibility is pathetic, especially in comparison to the voter turnout of most other democracies around the world, which frequently exceeds 80%.[107] Even more indicting, in Iraq's second presidential election since the fall of Saddam Hussein, voter turnout exceeded 63%.[108] This was in spite of the fact that countless acts of violence and terrorism were performed to intimidate voters from participating in the fragile new democracy. A greater percentage of Iraqis voted in their second presidential election, *even under the threat of*

---

[a] For the reader's convenience, it should be understood that when most political commentators reference the "historic nature" of Barack Obama's election in 2008, they are alluding to the unfortunate fact that the main reason for the dramatic increase in voter turnout was because Obama was the first black man to run for president, thus increasing the voter turnout in the black community. Even Leftists are hesitant to brag that race was the main reason for the increase in voter turnout.

Civic Duty

death, than Americans have ever voted in any presidential election since 1960 (with the anomalous exception of 2008).

As usual, the numbers for Millennials are worse. Even at the height of Millennials' Obama-worship in 2008, voter turnout only reached 51%. Only *half* of Millennials voted –and that was nearly a record![109] Conversely, more than two-thirds of seniors vote regularly in presidential elections. By not voting, Millennials voluntarily disenfranchise themselves, which is akin to a self-imposed tyranny. If we don't vote our interests, how can we complain when the government raises taxes in order to pay for seniors' Social Security and Medicare? How can we complain when we get out of college and can't find a job? Will we really be content to allow the government to load us down with the burden of paying for the entitlements of the elderly, the poor, and needy when we ourselves are struggling to find work after graduating? How long will we let the government punish us for the irresponsibility of others?

Surely, the apathy of my generation is perhaps one of the most dangerous threats to our freedom. I grew up with it in high school and experienced it on a daily basis. People just don't care about the health of our nation's political and moral fiber. Even worse, those that do care don't have the tenacity to get up and say something about it –mostly for reasons discussed in the earlier chapters of "Intellectual Independence" and "Moral Courage." Students are afraid of social ostracism and administrative

First Principles for my First Election

discipline if they dare think for themselves –or even worse, act on those thoughts and exercise their first amendment rights! We are told time and time again that the system is rigged, the elites know best, and that the man is keeping us down. We are told that we can't make a difference.

We can not underestimate how severely this attitude of learned helplessness limits the future opportunities of our generation. 18th century philosopher Montesquieu said it himself, "The tyranny of a prince is not so dangerous to the public welfare as the apathy of a citizen in a democracy."[110] If the government can condition our generation, like the mindless lab rats they think we are, to feel helpless and incompetent to solve the problems of the world's tomorrow, then we ourselves have accomplished the tyranny they so desperately seek to impose on us. Government is supposed to be a servant to the People, its master. However, if the master is silent, then who is to control the servant? Who will stop the servant from becoming the master?

Though this pandemic of apathy is indeed the greatest threat to our freedom, I believe that it is the most easy to remedy. As I have said before, I believe in the creative potential of my generation. Though we have been born into trying times, our problems are not new ones. The threat of economic collapse, moral decay, and cultural decadence are not new problems in the history of man. However, the tools we have at our disposal to solve these antiquated dilemmas are unprecedented and powerful

Civic Duty

beyond measure. With the explosion of technological innovations in the 21st century,[b] we have at our fingertips the means to change the world! No longer do the media have a monopoly on information and free speech. Instead of three news networks, we now enjoy cable, internet, blogs, and social media as means of receiving information and broadcasting our ideas. This is a fantastic opportunity to engage in the public discourse. As Millennials, we have the advantage of being techno-savvy and can build for ourselves a powerful voice on the net.

Again, take for example TheCollegeConservative.com blog, of which I am now a contributor. What started with one person's idea and imaginative spirit grew to a group of ten, and then 20, and now 50 writers who have reached an audience of more than 1,000,000. That one internet blog has united all 50 of our staff members –all conservative college students- and has shown us that we are not alone in our fight to restore truth and beauty to public life. We have also been able to broadcast our traditional values and political principles of free-market capitalism and individual liberty to the entire world without fear of persecution from school administrators or government regulations. That is the power of technology in the 21st century America!

---

[b] Note that this "explosion" of technological innovation was not just some magical phenomenon. It was the natural culmination and economic consequence of the American political structure that has embraced the principles of free-market capitalism and allowed the genius of man to create, innovate, and explore the depths of his imagination.

First Principles for my First Election

Obviously, the conservative understands that technology is merely a tool, an instrument. It has no intrinsic value in itself and can be used for either good or evil. It can just as easily be used in the advocacy of tyranny as liberty. The election of President Obama in 2008 is case in point.

In the historic election of 2008, the percentage of people using the internet for political activism increased sharply by 21% from the last election just four years prior.[111] The Pew Research Center conducted many studies that found that young people were more likely to watch political videos, share/forward election news, engage politically on a social networking site, etc.

Civic Duty

Among politically engaged internet users, young adults have the highest level of involvement

Online activities among online political users (the 55% of the voting-age population who used the internet in one way or another for political purposes during the 2008 campaign)

	18-29	30-49	50-64	65+
% who are online political users	72%	65%	51%	22%
These activities are engaged in by a range of age groups				
Watch online political videos	67	62	54	40
Share/forward political or election news	44	44	41	47
Young online political users dominate these activities				
Engage politically on a social networking site	49	22	7	2
Post original content related to the campaign	40	21	17	9
Customize political or election news	32	21	19	15

Source: Pew Internet & American Life Project Post-Election Survey, November-December 2008. Margin of error is +/-3% based on online political users.

Pew Internet
Pew Internet & American Life Project

First Principles for my First Election

Millennial generation was exploited by the Obama campaign machine which target the youth vote early on in the election cycle. In every category of online volunteerism, Obama supporters were able to outperform McCain supporters –from forwarding texts, posting online, sharing video and news clips, etc.[112]

This example shows how powerful technology can be in enabling Millennials to engage in the political arena. However, it also shows how damaging technology can be to a generation not

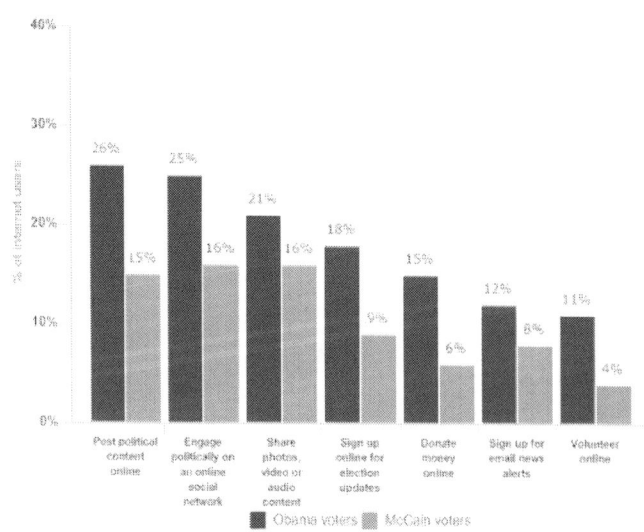

Civic Duty

grounded in universal principles of liberty and justice. Our generation fell for the enchanting demagoguery of candidate Obama in 2008, but we cannot allow our creative talents and unique abilities on the net to be exploited by him again. Now he is President Obama. He has a record, and a dismal one at that. It's time to shift our energy and creative passion away from his utopian promises of "hope" and "change," and to put our first amendment rights to good use.

    I encourage every Millennial to become actively involved in this election cycle and those to come. Never underestimate the power you wield and the influence you have in the political arena. The creation of cyberspace has opened up countless opportunities for Millennials to engage in the public discussion. Utilize those tools available to you! If freedom is to be maintained against the onslaught of an oppressive and expansive government, then we must adapt to the changing nature of the political atmosphere. In order for liberty to remain competitive in the war of ideas, we must take our cause to cyberspace –the last true bastion of man's independence.

    Engage your friends on Facebook. Create groups online and network with those who share your values. I promise that you are not alone! Tweet articles that you read, share political videos on social networking sites, SPEAK WITHOUT FEAR!

    Aside, from the many technological outlets for involvement highlighted above, there are countless other ways to

First Principles for my First Election

get make an impact in the war of ideas. As a teenager I have been extremely involved in my community. I have already written about my leadership of my high school's Young Conservatives. I have mentioned how we invited numerous guest speakers such as our state representative, state senator, county commissioner, and many others to have a dialogue with us. In addition to my leadership at school, I have also made an effort to seek out other means of involvement. I interned one summer for Lt. Governor Ron Ramsey who ran for governor of Tennessee in 2010, and I have volunteered on countless local campaigns. I regularly attend political events hosted by the Republic Party of Williamson County, the Heritage Foundation, Linchpins of Liberty, and ACT! for America. This gives me a chance to meet and greet the movers and shakers of the community. I'll never become a politician, but these experiences allow me to see first-hand what the political atmosphere is really like and gives me many opportunities to listen to inspiring speakers. It gives me the satisfactory feeling that I am educating myself, getting involved, and most importantly, making a difference.

    I say all this not to glorify myself, but to encourage you, the reader. Opportunities like those listed above are available to almost anyone! You just have to know where to look. Reach out to the organizations in which you have an interest. More than likely, civic, moral, and political organizations offer *huge* financial discounts to attract young people who might be willing

Civic Duty

to attend. I have been able to see many dignitaries such as Gov. Scott Walker of Wisconsin and Edwin Meese III (Chief Advisor to President Reagan) for little to nothing compared to the pretty penny that most adults were charged to go to these events. The key is to look for the opportunities yourself. Look for student discounts and if you are unsure if a meeting or event offers them, simply ask! Most importantly, form relationships with adults who are involved in your field of interest, not simply because you want another political "connection," but because you really desire to form a relationship with someone who shares your values and has the experience and tools to help you learn how to defend them. Many people that I have met in the course of my civic participation have turned out to become some of my closest mentors and family friends. Networking is important on a political level, but the importance of forming relationships on a principle level can never be underestimated.

  Political campaigning is also a great outlet for Millennials to expend some of our youthful energy. Local campaigns love to hire young people as volunteers, interns, and in some cases part-time employees. Whether it is phone-banking, knocking on doors, or making yard signs, you are sure to be put to good work if you decide to volunteer on a local campaign. All it takes is one phone call or one email to a candidate's campaign office. This is an excellent way to make a direct impact on your community and to have a little fun as well. From experience, political activism can

First Principles for my First Election

be extremely rewarding when you volunteer with some friends from school. It allows you to socialize while simultaneously bonding around a set of shared principles –and as an added benefit your resume will look much more attractive! Institutions of higher education and employers love to see that an individual has demonstrated the ability to be dedicated and passionate about something greater than him.

Self-government is no easy task. It requires active involvement by an engaged citizenry. Find your niche in society. Whether you are a blogger or a writer, a candidate or a campaigner, an educator or a student, you can be a leader in your family and in your community and an outspoken advocate for the restoration of first principles. Find that niche and fulfill your obligations to the utmost of your ability. We can't all be politicians –God forbid it if we were! We all can, however, be good citizens and good stewards of the liberty we so richly enjoy in this country. Citizenship is a duty, a duty which requires that each and every one of us work to our fullest potential.

I also encourage you to join me in the counter-culture revolution for civility! Part of our responsibility in civic engagement is to be decent, to respect each other as human beings rather than dehumanized partisan zombies. Unfortunately, it has now become mainstream in our culture to be rude and crude, whether talking about politics or not. Though the Washington Times finds that liberals are 12 times more likely than

Civic Duty

conservatives to use profanity in the blogosphere, both groups are guilty of throwing common decency out the window when exercising their free speech.[113] I encourage my fellow Millennials to change the culture on the net.

In the pursuit to unleash our wild and passionate spirits on the internet in the form of political activism, we cannot let our speech go completely unbridled. We must carefully monitor our own speech, to ensure that it is indeed civil and morally respectable, lest our anger and arrogant hubris do more harm than good to the cause of liberty. What shall others say if we fail to live by our own moral standards?

Not only do I consider the maintenance of proper decorum and decency a civic responsibility, but I also believe that maintaining civility and respect online is intrinsically beneficial to our cause. By self-regulating our own free speech, we create a stark contrast with our adversaries who more often than not resort to ad homenim attacks, stereotypes, and rude put-downs rather than solid principles when challenging the champions of liberty on the net. This contrast will make our argument even more attractive to those who are still testing the waters of political activism, and will even strengthen our belief in the moral necessity of responsible free speech in a civil society. In the words of the apostle Paul, "Don't let anyone look down on you because you are young, but set an example for the believers in speech, in conduct, in love, in faith and in purity (I Tim. 4:12)." Above all, adhere to

First Principles for my First Election

that old conservative virtue of prudence, espoused by the great statesman Edmund Burke. Choose your battles wisely, and when you do choose them, execute them effectively with words that accurately communicate the deep sentiments of liberty in a tone that is admirable and worthy of imitation.

It must be said, however, that no matter how fearless in speech, no matter how civil in conduct, no matter how brave in battle, all is for not if we forsake the principles outlined in this book. It won't matter how many of us vote, door-knock, phone-bank, or campaign in the coming election if we are not grounded in the first principles which I have now thoroughly explored. If all our energy is misdirected and abused by forces that oppose individual liberty and pervert social justice, as it was in the election of 2008, our efforts will be for naught.

Civic duty is a virtue, but it can easily become a vice; indeed, when involvement in politics becomes an end in itself, civic duty can become one of the most destructive forces to the civil society. What does this look like? Well, just look around. The political atmosphere of our society is corrupted by blind allegiance to political parties instead of a thoughtful dialogue. Politicians are more often prideful, dishonest, and self-serving rather than true statesmen of honor and integrity. Most who are involved in politics are involved for the wrong reasons –being motivated by money and power rather than patriotic duty. This dismal political atmosphere suffocates leadership, silences

Civic Duty

creative voices, and dampens the burning fire of youthful energy in this country. It has led many Americans to view politics and involvement in government as a "bad" thing, and thus has resulted in thousands, if not millions, of honorable Americans from shunning the system altogether.

This perception must change. We need not ignore the corruption, but at the same time, we cannot simply sit around twiddling our thumbs waiting for the next George Washington to appear out of thin air. Political commentator Glenn Beck regularly insists, and rightfully so, that we need to prepare ourselves and our families to become the next George Washington.[c] This country needs more honorable men and women who have the honesty and integrity to hold public office. It also needs more honorable men and women who will live out their morals in the private sector, who will actively participate in their own governance so that their freedom and their children's freedom will be preserved.

Truly, civic participation should be the natural extension of the first principles outlined thus far. If one has truly liberated his mind by declaring intellectual independence, if one has resurrected the idea of moral imagination and the courage to defend it, if one has been inspired by the creative forces of entrepreneurship and self-reliance, and if one has a firm belief in

---

[c] I recommend reading Glenn Beck's book *Being George Washington*, which reads like a novel and allows the reader to meet the *real* George Washington who was just as human as you and me.

First Principles for my First Election

America's exceptionalism, he should be *glad* to participate in a free society!

Millennials have been injected into a point in history that is sorrowfully lacking in solid, foundational principles. The good news is that we have the opportunity to bring fresh blood into the dying pulse of American culture. We can transform the conscious of the American mind by the renewal of our founding fathers' first principles. We can also begin to reorder the spiritual soul of our nation by restoring the idea that God is the ultimate granter of our liberty and prosperity, not the government. This will be accomplished through the fulfillment of our civic duties.

As we struggle to translate these principles into sound public policies, I beg my fellow Millennials to remember the words of President Ronald Reagan who warned against moderation in the public arena, stating that the only way to political victory was by "raising a banner of no pale pastels, but bold colors which make it unmistakably clear where we stand on all of the issues troubling the people…It is time to reassert our principles and raise them to full view. And if there are those who cannot subscribe to these principles, then let them go their way."[114]

That statement is in itself bold, but when put into its historical context, its meaning is all the more powerful. Ronald Reagan made these comments in a speech at the Conservative Political Action Committee (CPAC) on March 1st, 1975. The Republican Party had just experienced a horrible election outcome

Civic Duty

in light of Nixon's Watergate Scandal. The party suffered from bad public opinion and seemed to be internally wounded beyond repair. Republicans still loyal to the party viciously debated what direction to take the party going forward. Some argued that it should moderate its position on many issues so it could broaden its base and attract more members.[d] Reagan saw these moderate proposals as a direct threat to his beloved principles.

This speech became famous for Reagan's insistence on a political party built by strong principles, or what he called bold colors not pale pastels. He knew that the survival of his principles –which included a dedication to individual liberty, free market capitalism, moral certitude, and a "peace-through-strength" foreign policy, was more valuable than the popularity of any political party. As it turned out, this stubborn adherence to principled public policies ended up winning him the presidency five years later. In one of the nation's most dramatic landslide elections, Ronald Reagan won 44 out of the 50 states in the Union with his positive message of principled conservatism. His election (and reelection) proved that the American people actually prefer bold colors to pale pastels. His success proved that people respond positively to someone who can articulate their foundational principles with command and authority. Unfortunately, the conservative movement to restore first principles has yet to find an equal to "The Great Communicator."

---

[d] This is often referred to as the "big-tent" philosophy.

First Principles for my First Election

This is the primary challenge for the rising generation. Once we have reconnected with our history and our heritage to rediscover our first principles, we must develop the eloquence and imagination to communicate them to all Americans, including our fellow Millennials. Just as Reagan did, we must rely on the boldness and audacity of our proposals to win legitimacy and authority in the public arena. Only by drawing a stark contrast between liberty and tyranny, truth and error, right and wrong will we be victorious.

This past summer was the first time I had the wonderful opportunity to visit Washington D.C. Though we could only afford to stay for three days, my family eagerly made the nearly twelve hour trip by car to get there; as we soon found out, the long trek through the rolling hills of East Tennessee and Blue Ridge Mountains of Virginia would be totally worth it. As a family we had hardly stepped foot out of the southeastern United States; needless to say, we were in for a treat.

For a history buff like me, the experience was even more overwhelming. The beautiful art and architecture that dominated our nation's capital was breath-taking. Never in my life had I ever glimpsed such beauty. Surely, the elegant grandeur of the art and architecture reflected the immense power and depth of meaning behind our country's most sacred monuments and historical buildings.

Civic Duty

The reading room of the Library of Congress had the most emotional impact on me by far. A gigantic room full of books, desks, reading lamps and its towering ceiling complete with sculptures and artwork of all kinds was home to the world's biggest library and largest collection of knowledge, history, and literature in human history. I also toured the Smithsonian (though I only had time to see a glimpse of the wealth of historical collections stored away in its many museums). I stood on the steps of the highest court in the land and I peered through the gates that surrounded the White House. I circled around the fountain of the WWII memorial, and I couldn't help but feel an up-swelling of gratitude for the thousands who gave their lives for freedom. I saw families at the wall of the Vietnam War memorial placing letters, flowers, and family memorabilia beneath the engraved name of their loved ones. On the steps of the Lincoln memorial, I could do nothing but stand in speechless awe. In front of me sat the man whose burdens during the Civil War were no doubt greater than the weight of marble that now eternally enshrine the memory of his sacrifice. Behind me, overlooking the steps of the Lincoln memorial and the long reflecting pool, towered the obelisk monument dedicated to our nation's first president, George Washington.

All around me was the history and legacy of a mighty empire –an "empire of liberty." Evidence of its heroes and their victories was on every corner. All of this I pondered one evening

First Principles for my First Election

as my family sat on the edge of the reflecting pool in front of the nation's capitol building waiting for the sunset. A paradox of emotions filled me as my gaze wandered over the still water reflecting the mirror image of the capitol. There, I knew, was the place they took away our liberty. There was the place that turned history and precedent on its head replacing them instead with overconfidence in the mind of the modern man and the "progressive" notions that guide his unstable world view. How, I wondered, could this great place steeped in so much tradition and honor become the strongest foothold for the advocates of unrestrained centralization? The place which used to stand for ordered liberty and religious freedom now serves as a world symbol for corruption and moral anarchy. I knew that if my country was to be preserved, my generation, the Millennials would be the ones to do it, but we would have to start now. If Washington D.C. is ever to return to its former glory, if the federal government is ever to return to its proper function as an institution of collective security and promoter of civil society, rather than a tyrannical force led by overeducated and self-righteous politicians, Millennials must act.

The 2012 election will be our first opportunity to show the nation that we mean business. Defeating President Obama must be priority number one. His mantra of "hope and change" has become the punch line of the joke that is the state of our union. As stated in the introduction to this manifesto, his policies have failed

Civic Duty

at home and abroad. Under his administration, the forces of radical Islam remain stronger than ever. He has encouraged revolution and instability in the Middle East in the name of "democracy" and "freedom," but this has only led to more chaos and insecurity for Israel and the United States. Iran is closer than ever to developing nuclear weapons. All the while, we lead the world from behind as we continue to surrender our sovereignty to international organizations such as the U.N. On the domestic front, the economy continues to suffer from the crushing burden of debt, regulation, and taxation. Entitlements have enslaved more Americans to dependence on government than at any point in recorded history. Little hope exists for the leaders of tomorrow so long as the public education system and institutions of higher learning continue to function as centers of liberal indoctrination and social experimentation rather than as places where students can pursue worldly and spiritual Truth.

    We must oppose President Obama this Fall not because he is a Democrat, but because both his record and his rhetoric contradict the very principles on which this country was founded. He and his party stand for the status-quo in education. They favor the power of teachers unions over the interests of students; they stand for political correctness over the freedom of expression; and they promote indoctrination rather than intellectual independence. The President's party makes a mockery of religious liberty in their "progressive" attempts to eradicate faith from the public arena.

First Principles for my First Election

The President and his party believe that government is the creator of wealth, rather than private entrepreneurs; and they punish the self-reliant citizens of society through progressive taxation which redistributes wealth. We must oppose President Obama because his policies are unsustainable for a healthy society that wishes to remain free.

    Yes, exercising our civic duty to defeat President Obama is the first step; however, the path to restoring America goes far beyond politics. Whatever the outcome of the election this November, Millennials must stay vigilant in the rediscovery and resurrection of our first principles. Whichever candidate wins we must stay the course by continuing to develop as individuals, both physically, intellectually, and spiritually. We must connect with our history and heritage and discover what makes us unique as a people, what makes us exceptional. We must develop the moral imagination to "orient ourselves in the existence of a divine creation" by growing closer in our relationship with God and maintaining a healthy curiosity about the unseen world –learning to meditate on things of eternal nature rather than the sensual world around us. We must develop as self-reliant individuals, learning to live independent of our parents and free from government control. We need to develop the creative faculty of entrepreneurship so that we can find our niche in society and leave things better than they way we found them. Finally, we need to become involved in the political process –hopefully through

Civic Duty

defeating the administration in power and holding the feet of the next one to the fire. In a society lacking both in spirit and flavor, we need to be the bold colors that liven up the picture of America's future.

What an exciting time it is to be alive! The world is changing faster than at any time in human history, and we Millennials are smack-dab in the middle of it. Though civilization seems to be eroding on an economic and spiritual level before our very eyes, our generation has the ability, creativity, and resources to reverse that trend and to transform America into something greater than ever before. This won't be accomplished, of course, through politics or progressive principles like "social justice," which simply amount to a set of phony, feel-good political policies. Neither will it be accomplished by radical ends, though disenchanted souls such as the Occupiers insist on tearing down the whole system. No, America will be made new by destroying her. "Men cannot improve a society by setting fire to it; they must seek out its old virtues, and bring them back into the light."[115]

Sure, change will come. "Change in society is natural, inevitable and beneficial; the statesman should not try vainly to dam the whole stream of alteration, because then he would be opposing Providence." Our goal as Millennials living in this revolutionary time period should be to lead the "waters of novelty into the canals of custom."[116] In other words, as we move forward as a nation, we must necessarily adapt to the new political and

First Principles for my First Election

social environment in which we find ourselves, but we must learn to be a generation that will force any change that comes to be in conformity with our first principles and the values that we hold dearest to our hearts. "Our part is to patch and polish the old order of things, trying to discern the difference between a profound, slow, natural alteration and some infatuation of the hour."[117]

As my preacher is fond of saying, "We live in a mixed-up, messed-up world." Truth is forsaken for general relativity, and morality is turned up-side down. Chaos and lawlessness reign, while only a righteous remnant remains to defend what is Noble and True. We the Millennials must be the voice of reason in a world that is slipping down the path of no return. Drawing on the strength of our heritage, our tradition, and Almighty God, it is time to return to our first principles.

Appendix:

Suggested Reading for the Rising Generation

It would be foolish for me to encourage the declaration of intellectual independence and moral certitude without also providing my reader with some direction. Throughout this book I have made a conscious effort to reference great books and genius thinkers who have contributed to conservative thought. However, I could hardly mention every book or author worthy to be read. Therefore, I have included the following selection as an extended list of books which have influenced my thinking and sparked my imagination in the quest to discover my first principles. While this list is by no means exhaustive, I believe it is sufficient to start any curious Millennial on the path to understanding ordered liberty. Enjoy!

History	**Moral Imagination**	**Modern Political Culture**
The Roots of American Order -By Russell Kirk	*Mere Christianity* -by C.S. Lewis	*Liberty and Tyranny* -by Mark Levin
The Conservative Mind -by Russell Kirk	*Miracles* -by C.S. Lewis	*Sharia Law for Non Muslims* -by the Center for the study of Political Islam
George Washington's Sacred Fire -By Peter A. Lillback	*The Screwtape Letters* -by C.S. Lewis	*Common Sense* -by Glenn Beck
Liberty and Learning -by Dr. Larry Arn	*From Darkness to Great Light* -by Galina Koval	*Demonic* -by Ann Coulter
48 Liberal Lies about American History -by Larry Schweikart	*The Purpose Driven Life* -by Rick Warren	*Godless* -by Ann Coulter
American Progressivism -by Ronald J. Pestritto, William J. Atto	*The Science of God* -by Gerald L. Schroeder	*Guilty* -by Ann Coulter **Autobiography** *My Grandfather's Son* -by Clarence Thomas

About The Author

ALAN GROVES, 18, recently graduated from Ravenwood High School in Williamson County, TN. He is now a Law and Politics major at Freed-Hardeman University. He is a contributor for *TheCollegeConservative.com*, a member of the College Republicans, a board member of the civic organization Linchpins of Liberty, and a member of the Heritage Foundation.

Visit his website at:
http://firstprinciplesformyfirstelection.blogspot.com/

Notes

Notes - Introduction

[1] (n.d.). Retrieved from http://www.usdebtclock.org/

U. S. Department of Labor, Bureau of Labor Statistics. (2012). *Household data: Table a-1. employment status of the civilian population by sex and age* . Retrieved from website: http://www.bls.gov/news.release/empsit.t01.htm

[2] Tompson, T. (2010, October 13). College students' obamania wanes: Ap-mtvu poll. *The Huffington Post*. Retrieved from http://www.huffingtonpost.com/2010/10/13/college-students-obamaman_n_761410.html

Deyen, D. (2010). *The youth vote: Still pro-democratic, turnout average for a midterm election.* Retrieved from http://news.firedoglake.com/2010/11/03/the-youth-vote-still-pro-democratic-turnout-average-for-a-midterm-election/

[3] Ray, J. (2011, March 11). *U.S. leadership approval loses some momentum worldwide.* Retrieved from http://www.gallup.com/poll/146555/Leadership-Approval-Loses-Momentum-Worldwide.aspx

Cooper, R. (2011, August 1). *Morning bell: Liberals force choice between economic and national security.* Retrieved from http://blog.heritage.org/2011/08/01/morning-bell-liberals-force-choice-between-economic-and-national-security/

Notes - Principle #1: Intellectual Independence

[4] Hernandez, R. (2007, December 20). It's not just 'ayes' and 'nays': Obama's votes in Illinois echo . *The New York Times*. Retrieved from http://www.nytimes.com/2007/12/20/us/politics/20obama.

Notes

html?_r=4

[5] A. Leiserowitz, E. Maibach, & C. Roser-Renouf, (2010) Climate Change in the American Mind: Americans' Global Warming Beliefs and Attitudes in January 2010: Yale University and George Mason University (New Haven, CT: Yale Project on Climate Change, http://environment.yale.edu/uploads/AmericansGlobalWarmingBeliefs2010.pdf

[6] Kirk, R. (2003). *The roots of American order.* (4th ed., p. 467). Wilmington, DE: ISI Books.

[7] Kurtz, H. (2005, March 29). College faculties a most liberal lot, study finds. *Washington Post.* Retrieved from http://www.washingtonpost.com/wp-dyn/articles/A8427-2005Mar28.html

[8] McManus, S. (2008, April 21). If god is dead, who gets his house?. *New York Magazine.* Retrieved from http://nymag.com/news/features/46214/

[9] Eberhard, J. (2004, January 29). *Liberal bias on campus.* Retrieved from http://commonsensegovernment.com/article-01-29-04.html

[10] Koval, G. (1996). *From darkness to great light: An American adventure with a Russian remembrance.* (p. 52). Brentwood, TN: Penmann Books.

[11] Arnn, L. P. (2004). *Liberty and learning: The evolution of American education.* (p. 12). Hillsdale, MI: Hillsdale College Press.

[12] Zellie, C. (2005, April). *John Dewey, pragmatism, and progressive education quotes.* Retrieved from

Notes

http://www.intellectualtakeout.org/content/john-dewey-pragmatism-and-progressive-education-quotes

[13] Weaver, R. (1948). *Ideas have consequences.* Retrieved from http://www.nyx.net/~kbanker/chautauqua/consequences.html

[14] Kirk, R. (2008). *The conservative mind.* (p. 255). BN Publishing. DOI: www.bnpublishing.net

[15] Mirkinsin, J. (2010, October 21). Juan Williams fired: NPR sacks analyst over fox news Muslim comments. *Huffington Post.* Retrieved from http://www.huffingtonpost.com/2010/10/21/juan-williams-fired-npr_n_770901.html

[16] Williams, J. (2010, October 21). *Juan Williams: I was fired for telling the truth.* Retrieved from http://www.foxnews.com/opinion/2010/10/21/juan-williams-npr-fired-truth-muslim-garb-airplane-oreilly-ellen-weiss-bush/

[17] Williams, J. (2010, October 21). *Juan Williams: I was fired for telling the truth.* Retrieved from http://www.foxnews.com/opinion/2010/10/21/juan-williams-npr-fired-truth-muslim-garb-airplane-oreilly-ellen-weiss-bush/

[18] Kirk, R. (2008). *The conservative mind.* (p. 387). BN Publishing. DOI: www.bnpublishing.net

[19] Kirk, R. (2012, June 5). *The end of learning.* Retrieved from http://www.imaginativeconservative.org/2012/06/end-of-learning.html

[20] *Jefferson's religious beliefs.* (n.d.). Retrieved from http://www.monticello.org/site/research-and-

Notes

collections/jeffersons-religious-beliefs

[21] *Samuel Adams quotes*. (n.d.). Retrieved from http://ushistorysite.com/sam_adams_quotes.php

[22] Kirk, R. (2003). *The roots of American order*. (4th ed., p. 14). Wilmington, DE: ISI Books.

[23] Kirk, R. (2003). *The roots of American order*. (4th ed., p. 132). Wilmington, DE: ISI Books.

[24] Engel v. Vitale (1962)

[25] Barton, D. (2001). *Sample letters to the editor*. Retrieved from http://www.wallbuilders.com/LIBissuesArticles.asp?id=113

[26] *The founders and public religious expressions*. (2000, January). Retrieved from http://www.wallbuilders.com/LIBissuesArticles.asp?id=121

[27] *The founders and public religious expressions*. (2000, January). Retrieved from http://www.wallbuilders.com/LIBissuesArticles.asp?id=121

[28] Lohan, T. (2011, August 6). *Do we need a militant movement to save the planet (and ourselves)?*. Retrieved from http://www.alternet.org/story/151918/do_we_need_a_militant_movement_to_save_the_planet_(and_ourselves)

[29] Sargent, M. (2009, April 21). *Left-wing extremist joins Osama on FBI most wanted list*. Retrieved from http://newsbusters.org/blogs/mike-sargent/2009/04/21/left-wing-extremist-joins-osama-fbi-most-wanted-list

Notes

[30] *Ecoterrorism: Extremism in the animal rights and environmentalist movements.* (2005). Retrieved from http://www.adl.org/learn/ext_us/ecoterrorism.asp?learn_cat=extremism&learn_subcat=extremism_in_america&xpicked=4&item=eco

[31] Hassard, J. (2012, April 23). *Creationism and intelligent design make stealth appearances in Louisiana and Tennessee science classrooms.* Retrieved from http://www.artofteachingscience.org/2012/04/23/creationism-intelligent-design-stealth-appearances-louisiana-tennessee-science-classrooms/

[32] *Scientists and belief.* (2009, November 5). Retrieved from http://www.pewforum.org/Science-and-Bioethics/Scientists-and-Belief.aspx

[33] Driscoll, E. (2012, July 4). *Beyond the theory of moral relativity.* Retrieved from http://pjmedia.com/eddriscoll/2012/07/04/beyond-the-theory-of-moral-relativity/

[34] *Issue 3: The case for god in the public square - the case for god in the public square .* (2012). Retrieved from http://www.foundingspirit.org/issues/5-case-for-god-in-the-public-square?start=1

[35] *Franklin's appeal for prayer at the constitutional convention.* (n.d.). Retrieved from http://www.wallbuilders.com/libissuesarticles.asp?id=98

[36] Barton, D. (2008). *The founding fathers on creation and evolution.* Retrieved from http://www.wallbuilders.com/LIBissuesArticles.asp?id=7846

[37] National Archives, (n.d.). *The charters of freedom.* Retrieved

Notes

from website: http://www.archives.gov/exhibits/charters/charters_of_freedom_14.html

[38] *The divorce rate is declining but still high.* (2010). Retrieved from http://www.familyfacts.org/charts/120/the-divorce-rate-is-declining-but-still-high

[39] *The proportion of married adults has decreased.* (2011). Retrieved from http://www.familyfacts.org/charts/150/the-proportion-of-married-adults-has-decreased

[40] Torre, S. (2011, February 10). *National marriage week: What the collapse of marriage means for children.* Retrieved from http://blog.heritage.org/?p=52022?query=National Marriage Week: What the Collapse of Marriage Means for Children

[41] Kirk, R. (2008). *The conservative mind.* (p. 47). BN Publishing. DOI: www.bnpublishing.net

[42] Kirk, R. (2008). *The conservative mind.* (p. 50). BN Publishing. DOI: www.bnpublishing.net

[43] Kirk, R. (2008). *The conservative mind.* (p. 390). BN Publishing. DOI: www.bnpublishing.net

Notes - Principle #3: Entrepreneurship

[44] *Light bulb: at a glance.* (2007). Retrieved from http://www.ideafinder.com/history/inventions/lightbulb.htm

[45] *Light bulb law a good or bad thing for America?* . (2011, February 21). Retrieved from http://pollingmatters.gallup.com/2011/02/light-bulb-law-good-or-bad-thing-for.html

Notes

[46] Matson, J. (2008, April 10). *Are compact fluorescent lightbulbs dangerous?*. Retrieved from http://www.scientificamerican.com/article.cfm?id=are-compact-fluorescent-lightbulbs-dangerous

[47] Matson, J. (2008, April 10). *Are compact fluorescent lightbulbs dangerous?*. Retrieved from http://www.scientificamerican.com/article.cfm?id=are-compact-fluorescent-lightbulbs-dangerous

[48] Gregg, S. (2011, July 04). 'real industrial entrepreneurs'. *National Review, LXIII*(12), 29.

[49] U.S. Census Bureau, Foreign Trade Division. (2010). *Top trading partners - total trade, exports, imports.* Retrieved from FTDWebMaster website: http://www.census.gov/foreign-trade/statistics/highlights/top/top1012yr.html

[50] *The no. 1 reason Americans want to work for themselves*. (2010, November 7). Retrieved from http://the-new-american-dream.com/2010/11/07/the-no-1-reason-americans-want-to-work-for-themselves/

[51] Kane, T. (2005, March 4). *Minimizing economic opportunity by raising the minimum wage.* Retrieved from http://www.heritage.org/research/reports/2005/03/minimizing-economic-opportunity-by-raising-the-minimum-wage?query=Minimizing Economic Opportunity by Raising the Minimum Wage

[52] Sowell, T. (n.d.). Interview by W.E. Williams [Web Based Recording]. Williams with Sowell: Minimum wage., Retrieved from http://www.youtube.com/watch?v=2jv1Zae0sgo

Notes

[53] Williams, W. E. (2003). *Congress's insidious discrimination.* Unpublished raw data, University of Economics, Retrieved from http://econfaculty.gmu.edu/wew/articles/03/insidious.html

[54] Adams, B. (2011, September 3). *Study seeks to explain disproportionately high unemployment numbers in black communities.* Retrieved from http://www.theblaze.com/stories/study-seeks-to-explain-disproportionately-high-unemployment-numbers-in-black-communities/

[55] Kirk, R. (2003). *The roots of American order.* (4th ed., p. 10). Wilmington, DE: ISI Books.

[56] Lips and McNeil. (2009, April 15). *A new approach to improving science, technology, engineering, and math education.* Retrieved from http://www.heritage.org/research/reports/2009/04/a-new-approach-to-improving-science-technology-engineering-and-math-education?query=a new approach to improving science technology engineering and math education

[57] OECD. (2009). *What students know and can do: Student performance in reading, mathematics and science.* Retrieved from http://www.oecd.org/pisa/46643496.pdf

[58] Lips and McNeil. (2009, April 15). *A new approach to improving science, technology, engineering, and math education.* Retrieved from http://www.heritage.org/research/reports/2009/04/a-new-approach-to-improving-science-technology-engineering-and-math-education?query=a new approach to improving science technology engineering and math education

[59] Armstrong, Cernan, and Lovell. (2011, May 24). Column: Is Obama grounding JKF's space legacy?. *USA Today.*

Notes

Retrieved from http://www.usatoday.com/news/opinion/forum/2011-05-24-Obama-grounding-JFK-space-legacy_n.htm

[60] Environmental Protection Agency, (1992). *The guardian: Origins of the EPA*. Retrieved from website: http://www.epa.gov/aboutepa/history/publications/print/origins.html

[61] Environmental Protection Agency, (1992). *The guardian: Origins of the EPA*. Retrieved from website: http://www.epa.gov/aboutepa/history/publications/print/origins.html

[62] Brownfield, M. (2011, November 29). *Morning bell: How the EPA may cost you thousands*. Retrieved from http://blog.heritage.org/2011/11/29/morning-bell-how-the-epa-may-cost-you-thousands/

[63] Katz, D. (2011, January 26). *Rolling back red tape: 20 regulations to eliminate*. Retrieved from http://www.heritage.org/research/reports/2011/01/rolling-back-red-tape-20-regulations-to-eliminate

[64] Saad, L. (2011, March 14). *U.s. oil drilling gains favor with Americans*. Retrieved from http://www.gallup.com/poll/146615/Oil-Drilling-Gains-Favor-Americans.aspx

[65] Newport, F. (2011, April 4). *Majority of Americans say nuclear power plants in U.S. are safe*. Retrieved from http://www.gallup.com/poll/146939/Majority-Americans-Say-Nuclear-Power-Plants-Safe.aspx

[66] Comby, B. (n.d.). *Why France produces 80% of its electricity with nuclear energy while it's only 15% in the us ?*.

Notes

Retrieved from http://www.ecolo.org/documents/documents_in_english/US15-80France-Nov-05.htm

[67] Young, A. (2004, September 7). *The origin of the income tax*. Retrieved from http://mises.org/daily/1597

[68] Lopez, L. (2011, June 23). *The ten states most friendly to business*. Retrieved from http://www.businessinsider.com/the-top-ten-states-for-low-taxes-and-business-friendly-regulation-2011-6?op=1

[69] *Texas leads nation in exports, job creation*. (2011). Retrieved from http://www.timesrecordnews.com/news/2011/feb/18/texas-leads-nation-in-exports-job-creation/

[70] *Top contributors to Barack Obama*. (2011, September 26). Retrieved from http://www.opensecrets.org/pres08/contrib.php?cycle=2008&cid=n00009638

[71] Carroll, C. (2008, June 16). *The U.S. does have world's second highest corporate tax rate*. Retrieved from http://blog.heritage.org/2008/06/16/the-us-does-have-worlds-second-highest-corporate-tax-rate/

[72] *Questions over Obama's off-the-cuff remark*. (2008, October 15). Retrieved from http://www.foxnews.com/story/0,2933,438302,00.html

[73] Brownfield, M. (2011, July 27). *Morning bell: Tangled up in washington's red tape*. Retrieved from http://blog.heritage.org/2011/07/27/morning-bell-tangled-up-in-washingtons-red-tape/

[74] Department of Labor, Office of Disability Employment Policy.

Notes

(n.d.). *Encouraging future innovation: youth entrepreneurship education.* Retrieved from website: http://www.deomi.org/diversitymgmt/documents/employment/Encouraging_Future_Innovation_Youth_Entrepreneurship_Educati.pdf

Notes - Principle #4: Self-Reliance

[75] *In fox news special called freeloaders, john stossel dresses up like a "beggar" and panhandles for change.* (2011, March 25). Retrieved from http://mediamatters.org/video/2011/03/25/in-fox-news-special-called-freeloaders-john-sto/177985

[76] *In fox news special called freeloaders, John Stossel dresses up like a "beggar" and panhandles for change.* (2011, March 25). Retrieved from http://mediamatters.org/video/2011/03/25/in-fox-news-special-called-freeloaders-john-sto/177985

[77] *Federal revenue and spending: Federal budget in pictures.* (2012). Retrieved from http://www.heritage.org/federalbudget/default

[78] *Federal revenue and spending: Federal budget in pictures.* (2012). Retrieved from http://www.heritage.org/federalbudget/default

[79] *How much are we spending on welfare programs?.* (2012). Retrieved from http://www.askheritage.org/how-much-are-we-spending-on-welfare-programs/

[80] Arnn, L. P. (2004). *Liberty and learning: The evolution of American education.* (p. 32). Hillsdale, MI: Hillsdale College Press.

[81] Bradley, K. (2010, June 24). *Confronting the unsustainable*

Notes

growth of welfare entitlements: Principles of reform and the next steps. Retrieved from http://www.heritage.org/research/reports/2010/06/confronting-the-unsustainable-growth-of-welfare-entitlements-principles-of-reform-and-the-next-steps

[82] Bradley, K. (2010, June 24). *Confronting the unsustainable growth of welfare entitlements: Principles of reform and the next steps.* Retrieved from http://www.heritage.org/research/reports/2010/06/confronting-the-unsustainable-growth-of-welfare-entitlements-principles-of-reform-and-the-next-steps

Notes - Principle #5 American Exceptionalism

[83] Jones, J. J. (2010, 12 22). *Americans see U.S. as exceptional; 37% doubt Obama does.* Retrieved from http://www.gallup.com/poll/145358/Americans-Exceptional-Doubt-Obama.aspx

[84] White, A. W. (2011, 07 11). [Web log message]. Retrieved from http://blog.heritage.org/2011/07/11/millennials-embrace-american-exceptionalism/

[85] Owen, L. O. (2012, 01 21). *What apple is wading into: A snapshot of the k-12 textbook business.* Retrieved from http://paidcontent.org/2012/01/21/419-the-abcs-and-123s-of-apple-and-the-k-12-textbook-market/ ; http://www.businessweek.com/bschools/content/aug2009/bs20090826_069900.htm
 ; Arndt, R. A. (2009, 08 26). *Paying for college textbooks for tightwads.* Retrieved from http://www.businessweek.com/bschools/content/aug2009/bs20090826_069900.htm

[86] Shaidle, K. S. (2008, 12 05). *Kwanzaa: violent 60s radical invented fake holiday.* Retrieved from

Notes

http://www.examiner.com/article/kwanzaa-violent-60s-radical-invented-fake-holiday

[87] Goldberg, J. G. (2012, 11 09). The bashing of American exceptionalism. *The Los Angeles Times*, Retrieved from http://articles.latimes.com/2010/nov/09/opinion/la-oe-goldberg-exceptionalism-20101109

[88] Lloyd, G. L. (n.d.). *The constitutional convention: Selected correspondence from summer 1787.* Retrieved from http://www.teachingamericanhistory.org/convention/correspondence.html

[89] Kauffmann, B. K. (n.d.). *James Madison "godfather of the constitution".* Retrieved from http://www.earlyamerica.com/review/summer97/madison.html

[90] Madison, J. M. (1788). The structure of the government must furnish the proper checks and balances between the different departments. *The Federalist No. 51*, Retrieved from http://www.constitution.org/fed/federa51.htm

[91] Kirk, R. (2008). *The conservative mind.* (p. 89). BN Publishing. DOI: www.bnpublishing.net

[92] Kirk, R. (2008). *The conservative mind.* (p. 86). BN Publishing. DOI: www.bnpublishing.net

[93] Kirk, R. (2008). *The conservative mind.* (p. 157). BN Publishing. DOI: www.bnpublishing.net

[94] Levin, M. R. (2009). *Liberty and tyranny: A conservative manifesto.* (pp. 160-161). New York, NY: Threshold Editions.

[95] Iran's nuclear program (nuclear talks, 2012). (2012, 07 31). *The*

Notes

New York Times, Retrieved from http://topics.nytimes.com/top/news/international/countries andterritories/iran/nuclear_program/index.html

[96] *Policy basics: Where do our federal tax dollars go?*. (2012, 07 12). Retrieved from http://www.cbpp.org/cms/index.cfm?fa=view&id=1258

[97] Brownfield, M. B. (2012, 05 02). [Web log message]. Retrieved from http://blog.heritage.org/2012/05/02/in-pictures-defense-spending-plummets-under-obamas-budget/

[98] Demint, J. D. (2010, 08 16). The new start treaty weakens u.s. national security. *U.S. News*. Retrieved from http://www.usnews.com/opinion/articles/2010/08/16/jim-demint-the-new-start-treaty-weakens-us-national-security

[99] Talent & Mackenzie, J. T. &. M. E. (2011). The dangers of defunding defense. *The Journal of International Security Affairs*, *20*, Retrieved from http://www.securityaffairs.org/issues/2011/20/talent&eaglen.php

[100] Talent & Mackenzie, J. T. &. M. E. (2011). The dangers of defunding defense. *The Journal of International Security Affairs*, *20*, Retrieved from http://www.securityaffairs.org/issues/2011/20/talent&eaglen.php

[101] Barton, D. B. (2000, 01). Treaty of tripoli *Wall Builders*, Retrieved from http://www.wallbuilders.com/libissuesarticles.asp?id=125

[102] Kirk, R. (2008). *The conservative mind*. (p. 415). BN Publishing. DOI: www.bnpublishing.net

[103] *Muslim brotherhood (1)* . (n.d.). Retrieved from

Notes

http://www.adl.org/terrorism/symbols/muslim_brotherhood_1.asp

[104] Lindley-French, J. L. F. (n.d.). *Libya: The transition clock.* Retrieved from http://www.ndu.edu/press/libya-the-transition-clock.html

[105] Kirk, R. (2008). *The conservative mind.* (p. 416). BN Publishing. DOI: www.bnpublishing.net

Notes - Principle #6: Civic Duty

[106] Kirk, R. (2008). *The conservative mind.* (p. 214). BN Publishing. DOI: www.bnpublishing.net

[107] *Voter turnout.* (n.d.). Retrieved from http://www.fairvote.org/voter-turnout

[108] Wright, R. W. (2005, 10 16). U.S. lauds voter turnout in iraq. *The Washington Post.* Retrieved from http://www.washingtonpost.com/wp-dyn/content/article/2005/10/16/AR2005101600301.html

[109] *New census data confirm increase in youth voter turnout in 2008 election.* (n.d.). Retrieved from http://www.civicyouth.org/new-census-data-confirm-increase-in-youth-voter-turnout-in-2008-election/

[110] *Trust for representative democracy quotes.* (n.d.). Retrieved from http://www.ncsl.org/legislatures-elections/trust/trust-for-representative-democracy-civic-educatio.aspx

[111] Smith, A. S. (2009, 04 15). The internet's role in campaign 2008. *Pew Research Center Publications,* Retrieved from http://pewresearch.org/pubs/1192/internet-politics-campaign-2008

Notes

[112] Smith, A. S. (2009, 04 15). The internet's role in campaign 2008. *Pew Research Center Publications*, Retrieved from http://pewresearch.org/pubs/1192/internet-politics-campaign-2008

[113] Sheffield, M. S. (2008, 08 07). Sheffield: Profanity greater on liberal blogs. *The Washington Times*, Retrieved from http://www.washingtontimes.com/news/2008/aug/07/profanity-greater-on-liberal-blogs/?page=all

[114] *Ronald Reagan stated in 1975, "raise a banner of bold colors, not pale pastels!"*. (n.d.). Retrieved from http://rmcpac.com/ronald-reagan-stated-1975-raise-banner-bold-colors-not-pale-pastels

[115] Kirk, R. (2008). *The conservative mind*. (p. 239). BN Publishing. DOI: www.bnpublishing.net

[116] Feulner, E. F. (2010, 08 27). [Web log message]. Retrieved from http://blog.heritage.org/2010/08/27/heritage-launches-the-center-for-policy-innovation/

[117] Kirk, R. (2008). *The conservative mind*. (p. 40). BN Publishing. DOI: www.bnpublishing.net

Made in the USA
Charleston, SC
17 August 2012